WINNING AT LOVE

The Alpha Male's Guide to Relationship Success

WINNING AT LOVE

The Alpha Male's Guide to Relationship Success

#40

MARTIN GRODER, M.D.

PAT WEBSTER, PH.D.

Bascom Hill Books

Bascom Hill Books
212 3rd Avenue North, Suite 290
Minneapolis, MN 55401
612.455.2293
www.bascomhillpublishing.com

ISBN - 978-1-935456-04-9
ISBN - 1-935456-04-0
LCCN - 2009910099

Cover Design by Jenni Wheeler
Typeset by Kristeen Wegner

Printed in the United States of America

Bascom Hill Books

TABLE OF CONTENTS

FOREWORD, BY PAT WEBSTER

Over a decade ago, my late husband Bill and I went into couples therapy with Marty Groder. As a therapist myself, and having been in individual therapy with Marty for a number of years, I thought I knew quite a bit about couples' relationships, about "getting those feelings out."

"We have to start over again, Pat," Marty said, not long into the session. "There are some things you've learned in therapy here that aren't going to work."

As Marty began helping me learn some of the tools that are outlined in this book, I was initially scornful. I had grown into young womanhood on the cutting edges of feminism. I studied to become a therapist and also began my own therapy in the early 1970s, when raw expression of emotion was encouraged. Having grown up in a family where emotions, especially anger, were discouraged, I struggled hard to learn to express my anger and set my own boundaries. Before I married Bill, I had been a single mom and working professional for twenty years. I had a black belt in karate. I knew how to stand up for myself. What was this polite stuff that Marty was trying to teach me? Manners Therapy? Was I to take training in becoming a fake?!

But I was in a stuck place in my marriage, and was paying to get unstuck. So I tried what Marty was offering. From the time we began using Marty's coaching up until Bill's death, we had one of our sweetest times together, and we had shared many sweet times. I wouldn't take anything for the ways in which I had learned to love and to be loved.

Some years later, in the beginning of a new relationship, I again sought Marty's help. He scribbled a diagram on a tablet page, explaining something about the particular nature of my struggle at the time. I stuck it in a file, and for the first time in years, looked at all the little pieces of similar papers I had accumulated over the years. I had a file full of nuggets of wisdom about couples' partnerships. Marty had done extensive research on leading edge literature about couples and emotions. Combining that knowledge with his many years of experience helping couples, he had evolved a theoretical structure that incorporates the tools he used so successfully in his professional work and in his own marriage. In my file were the little notes, building blocks that were part of the "house" of his theories.

I wanted to put the whole theory and structure into book form. I wanted to understand it more thoroughly for myself; I wanted it in my bones. I also had done extensive research into successful marriage and worked with couples in my clinical practice. I knew that a book that we could write could be helpful for others. For myself, and for the reader, I needed to make it simple. So I offered to join Marty in writing this book. It is his legacy to me; what we did together is a mutual legacy to the world.

I initially balked when Marty said, "You know, we have to write this book for guys." I'm not a guy, and I speak and write more easily to women. In response to my frown, Marty said, "Pat, how many women do you know who have twenty, thirty books on relationships?" "Lots." "And how many men (who are not professional colleagues) do you know who have *any* books on relationships?" "None."

"We need to write a book for alpha males about how to live in Loveland," Marty said. I overcame my initial hesitation about co-authoring a book for men; it helped that I am an alpha female, alpha traits honed by a difficult childhood, coming into young womanhood at the peak of feminism, and by being a single working mother.

The research and the construction of the basic model for this book were initially Marty's. The organization, simplification, and translation are mine. Along the way, I began to contribute in fleshing out and expanding the theory. I added material from my own research and experience. The book became ours. I have absorbed this material in my bones, though I still have to practice, a lot.

I feel deep gratitude to Marty, my mentor, friend and colleague. Thanks for your brilliance, your trust, your humanness and the fun- and for showing me again and again how to successfully use this material. Thanks for helping me to know more about loving and being loved. Thanks to Bud Harris, who, when I was in a time of being existentially adrift, encouraged me to move on my impulse to consider writing this book with Marty. Thanks to my daughter Ali, wise woman and gift to my soul, who has perhaps more than anyone taught me about love and forgiveness. I am grateful to my sister, Mary, for agreeing to incorporate these skills into our relationship and who blesses me regularly with her embodied big-heartedness. Thanks to all my friends, including the YaYa Sisters' movie club, who regularly ask me about the book and Marty's health and who have listened to me through the evolution of this writing project. Thanks to Marty's wife and my friend, Leslie, who agreed to share events of her precious marriage and also was a great editor. And thanks to my late husband, Bill, who gave one hundred percent to a loving, exciting, and sometimes challenging marriage.

Lastly, thanks to my Jay-Bear, for coming into my life.

FOREWORD BY MARTY GRODER

I had known peaceful, loving times. Peace, however, was episodic. My priorities were learning, productivity, winning when necessary, cooperating when possible. Eventually, I became relentlessly indomitable. I mounted the hierarchies of power. The U.S. Bureau of Prisons was building a research prison in Butner, N.C. I was made warden of the whole prison, charged with developing both the psychiatric program and the four research units.

I was thirty-two years old and, at that time, the youngest warden in the history of the Bureau of Prisons. I had the privilege of attending and participating in national wardens' conferences with men who had twenty to forty years of experience in prison work. I had only four years; but during that time, along with Wardens Pickett and Fenton, I quelled four major riots, without any injuries, in the major U.S. maximum-security prison. The last riot in 1972 was designed to precipitate a series of riots nationwide; we stopped it cold. I also constructed some innovative and effective programs, including Asklepieion, which reduced recidivism among volunteers with eighteen months in the program from 40-60% to 13%. And these were the hardcore homicidal maniacs. I was on a roll.

Then fashions changed. That happens, even in prison work. In April, 1975, I was out on the street, unemployed. All the power that seven years of hard work had given me was gone. The thousands who either loved or hated me were destined to become indifferent. At age 35, I was to become an urban legend.

As was my way then, I got mad. I vowed to get even. If I could not rule in Powerland, I would rule in "Who the hell knows?" But somewhere I would rule. I began to explore that which I will now call Loveland. In 1983 I realized that I could not stay in my first marriage and be in Loveland. So I left. After many years of hard searching and experimenting, and many failed relationships, I finally found myself living in Loveland fulltime. Paradoxically, ruling was not one of the choices. I had found the lovely, loving Leslie (whom I later married) to Sacagawea me the rest of the way to the Promised Land. (Sacagawea was the Native American princess who showed Lewis and Clark the way through her native land on their famous western expedition.) Leslie was a native speaker of Love and its ways: talk, action, wisdom and boundaries. I had never harmed her with my barbarian ways. I learned the full meaning of living in Loveland. I learned to live at peace with her and myself. I learned that my Warriors (see Chapter Six) were neither needed nor helpful in our home. I had become a naturalized citizen of Loveland. I began to teach what I know. Thus, this book.

Now, gentlemen, does this mean I have wimped out? No. I can and do strategize and act aggressively when necessary. Just NEVER at home. I also do not look for challenging fights with Giants. Fights interfere with being at peace. (As a young man, my motto had been: Kill a Midget, Eat for a Day; Kill a Giant, Eat for a Week!)

Pat Webster came along after a five-year sabbatical, during which time she had sailed off into the sunset, temporarily leaving her professional life. Pat and I have known each other for many years. She wrote her doctoral dissertation on the spiritual aspects of marriage and has had longstanding interest and skill in working with couples' relationships, incorporating my research and teaching. She was willing to do the hard work of organizing and writing the material; and as an alpha female, she understood the content. We have worked well together. While we have been writing this book, we were delighted to note the publication of Kate Ludeman and Eddie Erlandson's book, *Alpha Male Syndrome* (2006), about alpha males in the business world. We were excited to identify our alpha types in that book. I am a Visionary and Pat is an Executor; those two alpha aspects have teamed up well. Enjoy the result.

So, if you have failed at love enough and are sick and tired of being sick and tired and you are a Total Fucking Asshole like me (translation: high- functioning, arrogant, grandiose, leadership-type male), this book is for you. By the way, if you are an alpha female, this book is also for you. This book will be your GPS in Loveland to help you "recalculate" and get back on course. Good luck in using it; I hope you are not already in an irretrievably bad neighborhood.

I also want to thank the usual suspects. Thanks to Pat, who has earned a black belt in dealing with me. Thanks to Leslie, whom I love and have not harmed and who has built a safe haven with me. Thanks to my friends, colleagues, and last clients who have read this work and given it their best shot and love. Thanks to all helpers along the way. Acknowledgments go also to the women whose hearts I broke, including my ex-wife and mother of our children.

INTRODUCTION: SECOND CHANCES

This book is primarily for alpha males, or "top dogs." We'll talk more about that later; but let's just say that if you are a man and successful in the world of trade, business, or profession, most likely you are an alpha, or you have been trained to *act like* an alpha. You may be wondering how you can be so successful at your work but have failed in relationships.

It usually takes one or more significant failures before we become humble enough to think, "Maybe the failure had something to do with *me*." Only when we reach that place, and are lonely and hungering for relationship, do we become ready to examine our own behavior and attitudes and become willing, albeit reluctantly, to learn some new attitudes and skills that will prepare us for a more rewarding and lasting partnership. If you have not yet failed at one, two or more significant relationships, you may not be ready for this book. However, if you are smart, lucky and want to get ahead of the curve, you will read it anyway.

Occasionally, but not often, an alpha will be fortunate enough to experience this epiphany before having burned the last board in the bridge of his current relationship. Don't light that last fire! Rebuilding guidance is here.

For first marriages, the current divorce rate is 50%. For a second marriage, the divorce rate is between 66% and 75%, and it is even worse for third marriages. If you have failed in at least one marriage or significant relationship, it is important for you to know that you may have learned 70-80% of what you needed to know to make a relationship work, but *that's not enough*. While the 80% you *do* know is right and will be useful in a partnership, you are probably as passionately invested in the 20% that doesn't work as you are in the 80% that works. We know about this from our own former experiences. And a passionate investment in that 20% is enough to blow up a relationship.

You need a system that works, and that is not mystical or airy-fairy but a practical guidebook. If you are an alpha and living a life focused on achievement, making your way, surviving, you have three problems if you want love in your life on a continuing basis. In their book *Alpha Male Syndrome* (2006), about alpha males in the business setting, Kate Ludeman and Eddie Erlandson note that many alpha males have left a litter of failed marriages. Your first problem is that as an alpha male you may not know where love is. Second, even if you know where love is, you don't know how to get there. Third and worse yet, if you know where it is and if you get there, you are going to mess it up, especially under stress, because your natural instincts will lead you to turn away from love. This guidebook will help you solve those three problems. If you are interested, read on.

An Invitation to Alpha Females, Betas, and Those Interested in Improving Their Coupled Relationships

This book outlines the particular problems that alpha males encounter in personal relationships. We provide information on how to identify these problems and provide specific skills to work through them to create and deepen relationships that work and feel good to be in. The skills can provide an effective framework with real staying power. The advantages of being in a good relationship outweigh the advantages of not being in a relationship or of being in a dysfunctional relationship. Research has shown that couples in good marriages are in general healthier and live longer. The next healthiest group is single women; the next is couples in dysfunctional marriages, and at the bottom of the health totem pole is the group of single men. So guys, single women have a lot more to lose by pairing up with you, especially since most of them are, in this era, financially self-sufficient. And you have a lot to gain by learning to be in a healthy partnership, including better health and longer life.

We wrote the book for men. Except for Terrence Real, no one has written books for men about being in relationship in a language they can understand. Terrence does this in his book about depression in men, *I Don't Want to Talk About It* (1997). And because people with alpha qualities typically have more trouble in relationships than people with beta qualities, we wrote specifically for alpha males. We deliberately chose the structure, tone, voice, imagery, and examples with alpha males in mind.

We don't want to leave out alpha females and betas, however, and thus we have an invitation for you. About forty percent of females are alpha. The fastest and easiest way to identify alpha females is that they have higher than average testosterone levels and, in the absence of other mitigating circumstances (sexual abuse, trauma, etc.), easy and often quicker orgasms. They are also competitive, though will not admit it as readily as their male counterparts; sometimes they will even deny it. We will discuss alpha traits in the next chapter. Alpha females display many of the same traits as alpha males. However, in Ludeman and Erlandson's research (*Alpha Male Syndrome*, 2006, pp. 22-26), female alphas tend to utilize their alpha traits in the business world less destructively than do alpha males. Females also respond to stress by "tending and befriending," whereas the male response to stress is "fight or flight," ("UCLA Researchers Identify Key Biobehavioral Pattern Used by Women to Manage Stress," May 22, 2000, www.sciencedaily.com). In Ludeman and Erlandson's words, "...a great deal of wreckage is caused by boys behaving badly" (p.4). In our experience, the same is true in couples' relationships. As we discuss in Chapter Four, women have a genetic advantage in their neurological wiring and developmental fostering of relationships in early life training. They have an advantage in expressing emotions and being more sensitive to and empathetic with others. However, alpha females can also be unskilled in intimate partnerships and can cause relationship problems. If you are an alpha or beta male who is involved with an alpha female, you should both read this book.

People with beta characteristics have a natural affinity for connection and for being more constructive in relationships than do alphas. But that doesn't mean that they always have the skills or confidence necessary to create or to maintain healthy relationships. This may be especially true if they were parented by or have had adult relationships with unskilled alphas. Therefore, reading this book will be useful to them also.

If you are a reader not yet in your mid-forties, you may well be in a phase of your life cycle where career and ambition are still first priority. Or you may not yet have found a suitable partner with whom to practice these skills, either because you are single or because you are married to someone with whom it doesn't work to practice these skills. We suggest that you practice the material presented in the book in any relationship when at all possible. This might include relationships with close friends, family members, and your partner, when useful and appropriate.

Finally, some of our early readers have been in long-term (forty-plus years) successful marriages. They saw parts of themselves in the problem descriptions and found some of the tools and skills outlined in this book helpful. So, if you are one of these and looking for ways to polish up your marriage, we invite you to read the book also.

About Exercises, Foul Language, Pronouns, and Other Problems With Reading This Book

Some of our readers love the exercises that we have included. Some of our readers think they are at best not useful and at worst stupid. If you fall into the latter category, ignore them. If you like them, use them.

We use some foul language in the book. Some of our readers believe that this is unnecessary and offensive. They suggest that we substitute something like xx!!!!!/! and leave to the imagination the specific expletive. We chose to keep the language because this book is written for alpha men and women. Especially when alpha males have strong emotions, foul language ensues. So we chose not to clean up the language as some readers requested. We invite the squeamish not to read what they see on the page, instead see xx!!!!/! and allow your imagination to fill in the blanks. Likewise, in all the places in the book where it seems as if some tough guy is talking to you on a street corner in a bad neighborhood in New York, that's Marty's style. Just remember that he's an alpha brother and that you're getting friendly advice, just dressed in street talk.

Choosing when to use the pronouns "we" and "you" has been a tricky matter. One of our readers asked whether we were writing the book from the position of combination coach and schoolmarm (as when we use "you") or as one of the alphas who is speaking about his or her own TFA (Total Fucking Asshole) which is what we sometimes can be in relationships (as when we use "we"). The answer to the question is, yes. Sometimes we speak from our own experience and use "we." When we find ourselves speaking (from the position of our expertise in learning to address some of our TFA behavior) to our readers who might not yet know some of these things, we use "you." We ask you to bear with our choices.

Similarly, while the book is useful for alpha females, we have mostly used the pronoun "he" when referring to alphas. If you are an alpha female reading the book, and the material fits, please excuse our not using the awkward "he/she" pronouns.

Our species metaphors and relationship stories only cover some of the human potential. If the story or metaphor doesn't work for you, move on. One of the later stories will.

Our working assumption is that most male and female readers of this book have reached a place where sex is a pleasure and/or comfort and that they suffer neither sexual addictions nor any sexual behavior likely to cause personal, moral, professional, legal or relationship damage. We do not focus on the usual marriage breakers such as alcohol, infidelity, or violence. We address the issue of malice, and these marriage breakers are included under our definition of malice. We define malice as the intention and/or willingness to cause a partner harm. If you suffer from problems involving these afflictions, you will need to clean them up before this book will be helpful. Terrence Real addresses these in *The New Rules of Marriage* (2007, pp. 103-110).

The first part of this book is not easy to read because we talk about the problems of being an alpha male. The second part, in which we tell you how to fix relationship problems, is easier reading. We have to define the problem before we can talk about fixing it. It takes courage for any of us, especially alphas, to hear about liabilities that we bring to the relationship table. So, if you just can't read the first part, you can jump to the solutions and come back later, perhaps with some interest in understanding the basics. Or you can throw the book across the room, and go back to living your life in pain until you are ready to read it and take it in.

PART I: THE PROBLEM

CHAPTER ONE

THE CHALLENGE

We are both the problem and the only possible fixer of the miseries of love.

You, the alpha male, are both the problem and the only possible fixer of the miseries of love.

The most socially valuable skills of an alpha male are like the skills of the alpha in a wolf pack. The main function of the alpha is to protect the pack, to over-hunt, and to over-provide for members of the pack who are too young, too old, or too ill to hunt.

You are more than likely proud to be an alpha male. You should be. Ludeman and Erlandson (2006, p. 2) remind us that *alpha* is the first letter in the Greek alphabet and that "in English it has come to denote 'the first of anything'.... Animal researchers use the word to signify dominance, applying it to the leader of the pack, who is first in power and importance." Researched alpha attributes (Ludeman and Erlandson, 2006, pp. 11-12) include:

Dominance, confidence, a take charge attitude
Self-directedness
Goal-orientedness
Charisma
Aggressiveness
Competitiveness
High-achiever

Strong sense of mission
Bold, creative, innovative thinker
Persistence, tenacity, determination, steadfastness

In the workplace being an alpha is most often amply rewarded. Alphas are the guys who are known for getting stuff done.

For a man, surviving in the world requires that you either *are* an alpha, or learn how to act like one. If you are a beta male who has learned how to act like an alpha, your training may have occurred very long ago. You may have been acting like an alpha for so long, that you have forgotten that you are a beta, or you may feel confused about which you are.

Terrence Real, in his book *How Can I Get Through to You?* (2002), tells a poignant story about the early training of boys. His three-year-old son, Alexander, loved costumes. Sometimes he liked to dress as Kermit the Frog, sometimes as a wizard, sometimes as a bear and sometimes as Barbie the good witch. One day, as his five-year-old brother, Justin, was playing in the living room with several older friends, Alexander, in his excitement about the play date, decided to don his Barbie costume: white dress, silver wand, matching tiara. Here is Real's story as he tells it:

> Whooshing down the stairs he struck a magnificent pose for the big kids, like, "Ta-da!" The boys stopped their chatter and looked up, saying nothing. These boys were sensitive, liberal children and not a single word of open ridicule passed their lips. And yet, standing in the room with them, the moment felt molten. I sensed my own face burn red as Alexander turned heel, fled up the stairs, threw off the dress, jammed into a pair of jeans and, as casually as he could, joined the group as they retired downstairs to the woodshop to work on their swords, knives, and guns. That dress has never been touched again. (p. 78)

If you are an alpha male, and reading this, you may be thinking something like "Damn Straight!" The training begins really early.

Real continues:

> Without a shred of malevolence, the stare my son received transmitted a message: *You are not to do this.* And the medium that message was broadcast in was a potent emotion: *shame*. At three, Alexander was learning the roles. A ten-second wordless transaction was powerful enough to dissuade my son from that instant forward from what had been a favorite activity. I call such moments of induction the "normal traumatization" of boys.

> When I first began looking at gender issues, I believed that violence was a by-product of boyhood socialization. But after listening more closely to men and their families, I have come to believe that violence *is* boyhood socialization. The way we "turn boys into men" is through injury. We sever them from their mothers, research tells us, far too early. We pull them away from their own expressiveness, from their feelings, from sensitivity to others. The very phrase "Be a man" means suck it up and keep going. Disconnection is not fallout from traditional masculinity. Disconnection *is* masculinity. (p. 78)

It creates a big problem because, as an alpha, you are built and trained not to let others take advantage of you, not to let them hurt you. Survival is the point of all interactions. If they *do* hurt you, you are trained to get even, to teach them a bitter lesson. You are trained to hurt them in such a way that they will think twice before they ever try to hurt you again.

You do not blink first in a stare-down. You are trained to compete, and you are trained to win. If you are the *political* alpha, in the business world you do whatever is necessary to get a competitor out of the way. If you have information that he could use, you make sure he doesn't get it. If you must share information in order to *appear* cooperative, you keep some cards up your sleeve. If it looks as if he might be gaining ground toward a promotion that you both want, you know how to place a word of doubt about him that will work its way to the boss.

You are trained to be right, and if you are not right, to keep it hidden because winners don't make mistakes. Since you are right, you have difficulty listening to anyone else, unless it is to get enough information to turn it against them, to prove your point. You are not patient when someone disagrees with you, and why should you be? You are right, and you know it.

You are trained to suppress your emotions, unless it is the angry rage that you turn on someone who threatens you. When threatened, you feel immediately angry, and your first thought is how to eliminate the threat, or more to the point, how to either get rid of or "fix" the person who is threatening you. You may have murderous feelings toward that person, as evidenced by thoughts like, "I'm gonna kill that son of a bitch!" or, "He better not mess with me if he knows what's good for him." You are good at communicating those thoughts, even if you have to tone them down and do it subtly. You may even be good at charming others to agree with you so that they do not pose a threat to you; that is known falsely as charisma. See Phillip Rieff's book, *Charisma,* especially his definition of celebrity as spray-on charisma (2007, pp.3-13). You may be good at persuasion, arguing with others until they either agree with you or shut up.

Still not sure if you are one of us? Ludeman and Erlandson (and by the way, it should be clear by now that we recommend you read their book) have devised an Alpha

Assessment, based on their impressive research. To take advantage of their Alpha Assessment, go to www.AlphaMaleSyndrome/assessment. We recommend it because Ludeman and Earlandson's research regarding alpha traits has proved to be reliable and impressively valid.

While our own checklist has not had as much scientific validation, it is based on decades of personal and clinical experience. Some of the items are similar to the items in Ludeman and Erlandson's book (2006, p. 31). In order to get the best help from the remainder of the book, answer the following statements honestly by checking the ones that apply to you:

______ I was born to be a leader.

______ I often feel that my way is the best way.

______ I like to provide. It feels good to have people depend on me.

______ I am competitive.

______ I compare myself to others.

______ I don't give up until I reach my goal.

______ I seek out the company of other "winners."

______ I say exactly what I think, even if it hurts people's feelings.

______ I have strong opinions, both about things I know a lot about and things I don't need to know much about.

______ I have no problem challenging people.

______ When I face an adversary, my motto is "Intimidate, Dominate, Destroy."

______ Sex is scoring (for some, not all alphas).

______ I fight for my point of view.

______ I don't like it when people disagree with me.

______ I have high standards for myself and others.

______ I become annoyed when I have to listen to ideas that are inferior to mine.

_______ I have been told that I don't listen as well as I should.

_______ I find most people's conversations trivial and uninteresting.

_______ I give advice a lot.

_______ I solve people's problems, even when they haven't asked me to.

_______ Talk is a tool, to get my way. The techniques vary: over-talking, intimidating, harming, outfoxing.

_______ I easily become impatient with others, especially when I have to repeat myself.

_______ I FEEL aggressive. A lot.

_______ When someone displeases me, inconveniences me, or becomes aggressive, I feel that I have to do something. In the extreme, I feel like I want to do something *to* him or her.

_______ (For the more aggressive alphas), I carry a gun, sword or knife (real or imaginary), and I am ready to use my weapon at a moment's notice.

_______ When I get thwarted, I am tempted to end relationships. Thinking about ending relationships can give me a sudden jolt of feeling free. What I actually do with the feeling of wanting to end the relationship varies. I may actually end it. I may use the threat of ending it to attempt to intimidate and punish my partner. I may plan a sneakier form of revenge.

_______ The following question seldom comes to mind, and if it does, I most often answer in the negative: *Did I cause this?*"

If you answered yes to at least half of the above, you are most likely an alpha. Read this book for yourself, not for someone you know.

To determine if you are a beta, consider the following:

_______ I feel distressed if someone else is upset with me. I really want to find out why and work out a solution that works for both of us.

_______ I don't mind being a follower, especially if the leader is competent.

______ If I lead, I try to bring everyone along in the process.

______ It is not too hard to listen to another person's point of view, even if it is different from mine because differences are interesting.

______ I find it easy enough to put myself into others' shoes and understand them, even if I don't like their behavior or disagree with their point of view.

______ I see arriving at a mutually agreed upon solution as a process that takes time and patience.

______ The last thing I want to do is hurt someone.

You are a beta if you checked four or more of the above statements.

Powerland

You should have a clear idea by now whether you are an alpha or a beta. If you are an alpha, your highest values are about winning, being in charge, not being defeated, and having allies that are stronger than the enemy. "Achievement! Success! Total Victory at All Cost!" are your mottos. Love makes us vulnerable to loss. Marty's friend, Charlie Fenton, one of the great prison wardens of the twentieth century, had the following credo when Marty first met him: "Love or fear can bind a man to your heart. Fear is more reliable."

For the purposes of this book, we are going to give an imaginary name to the internal place in which you experience the attitudes, values, feelings and beliefs of the alpha: Powerland. Powerland can also exist in the real world. When people come from their internal Powerland and form communities or groupings, such as the workplace, the political arena, or the high-status country club, then external Powerlands are created.

Money is one of the sorting mechanisms for scorekeeping among alphas. Another sorting mechanism is level of skills in your profession, trade or business. Your score is enhanced by being rewarded with prizes and attention for those skills. Another sorting mechanism is being the best provider; your score increases when you are noted for that. Integrity is another sorting mechanism; the better your reputation, the higher your score. For some alphas in some social scenes, including bars, nightclubs, fraternities, and weddings, sexual scoring is a sorting mechanism ("Hey, man! How many times did you get laid last night?!"). The more you score, the more points you get. For first-responder-type alphas (firefighters, police, emergency technicians), being the most effective at helping others is a reward and sorting mechanism.

If you are an alpha, you were born in Powerland. You are a natural citizen of that inner place. You have learned how to live in Powerland, either because you like it and are rewarded for it or because you fall back to it when you are stressed. Survival is the point, *above all others,* in Powerland. Powerland never feels safe. It is a winner-take-all place. In Powerland, the highest values are about winning, being in charge, not being defeated and having allies that are stronger, faster and better than the enemy's allies. In Powerland, the most important thing is achievement. Love is something that gets in the way of that by weakening your resolve to triumph over all opposition. See Robert Greene's *The Forty-Eight Laws of Power* (2000), an exposition of total commitment to power.

In their research on alpha males' risks to organizations in the business world, Ludeman and Erlandson (2006, p. 12) include the following:

Intimidates
Creates fear
Stifles disagreement
Manipulates to get his way
Uses charm to lure people down his path
Competes with peers *(authors note: we substitute relationship partners)*
Gives others credit only reluctantly
Is arrogant
Is stubborn
Is overly opinionated
Imposes own views
Is closed to others' thinking
Drives self and others to exhaustion
Exudes urgency
Is impatient
Thinks rules don't apply to him
Launches into action before gathering support from others
Focuses so intently on future that present and near term are neglected
Is critical and demeaning
Fails to appreciate others' contributions
Has demoralizing effect on others

These same risks are present in intimate partnerships. And that is one reason why you, as an alpha male, have difficulty in relationships. The very skills that enable you to be a survivor in Powerland have concomitant risks. Those risks are a death knell to life in Loveland.

If we were to visually imagine Powerland, here's what it would look like. Imagine an island, laid out in an oblong fashion, west to east. Down the center of the island, running north to south is a swamp, separating the eastern half of the island from the western half.

The eastern half of the island to the right of the swamp is the Meadowlands. The Meadowlands is like a nice suburban development. This is where the sheepdog alphas live. It is inhabited by hardworking alpha males who have been properly brought up and socialized. Sheepdog alphas are fiercely protective of their families, hardworking, eagle-scout types. Here we find the carpenters, plumbers, firefighters, and other people who do a hard day's work honestly. What is missing is that they haven't made love and intimacy a top priority in their lives. They work shoulder-to-shoulder with everyone, including their spouses. The shoulder-to-shoulder model worked well until early into the twentieth century when all nations were primarily agrarian. There were so many honest people that you could leave your doors unlocked everywhere. Working shoulder-to-shoulder is important for obtaining mutual goals like survival and then perhaps a home in the Meadowlands, but does not foster deeper intimacy.

Over to the right or most eastern side of the Powerland island is a nice beach and sea channel between Powerland and Loveland. Loveland lies across the channel, east of Powerland. Ferries run between Powerland and Loveland. Sheepdog alphas can often easily ferry back and forth between Powerland and Loveland, though they live in the Meadowlands part of Powerland. They may visit Loveland during special times, such as an anniversary or a vacation but they are not natural citizens of Loveland. But if they cross the swamp separating Meadowlands from the western part of the island, they are in real trouble. This can happen when a sheepdog alpha wanders from Meadowlands. He gets into the muck because he gets ignited with some grand ambition or the desire for survival by whatever the means.

What's on the western end of Powerland? This end is a volcanic island. Because outlaws and low-level criminals, basically losers, unlike you, also use Powerland skills, down near the western shore of this end of the island are your classic bars and dives, where the low-level alphas live (e.g. loan sharks, pimps and drug dealers). This is a sleazy, seedy place. Slime runs down the hill.

Around the corner to the right of the sleazy-seedy port is a nice harbor, with lots of flashy marinas, country clubs, power yachts, and sleek high-speed boats used by very successful drug dealers. There is also an airport where runways await travelers who will jet in from Loveland. As we climb up from this sleek port we see wooded slopes. Here are the more rarefied abodes for people who have triumphed over almost everyone. Living here would be like living in a gated community. This isn't enough for everyone.

Part of the problem in Powerland is that if you are two-thirds up the mountain, you are drawn to be three-fourths up the mountain; when you are three-fourths up the mountain, you want to be seven-eights up the mountain, and so on. There is a fascination with going higher, being the best, outdoing all comers.

For the most ambitious, only getting higher, only getting to the top will do. What is higher? In the real world, higher might mean more money, more power, bigger promotions, golfing the best, making outstanding achievements in your field, political office, or securing a bigger contracting bid. Unfortunately, getting to the very top of Powerland is to get to the hole at the top of a dormant volcano. The hole is called a caldera, an empty hole that is rimmed, so that you can be seen by no one. This is the ultimate level in Powerland. It is a place of great isolation, surrounded by henchmen and cronies. No one can get to you, no one can influence you, and no one can tell you what to do. Other alphas are there to protect you. You need henchmen because all those skulls that you are sitting on have living relatives, neighbors, friends and allies who will be looking for you. You are unseen, hidden. When you come out to make a public appearance, your appearance is all staged, insulated, and surrounded by the protector alphas.

The caldera is the highest hole in the ground, where love is totally dead and absent. It is a very lonely place. Only a very few make it this high. Everyone at the top is inescapably paranoid because when people go this high, they become very insulated and isolated. In order to get here, the climber knows how he can be betrayed (because usually he has done those things on his way up), and he trusts someone either not at all or only so far. Information gets filtered to him through a very few reliable retainers and advisors, much like any dictator gets information. At this level in Powerland, the nagging discomfort is not about going higher because he has reached the top. Now, the discomfort is about staying on top, about protecting himself from people who are climbing the mountain who want to unseat him.

In order to get the job done and be rewarded in whatever is our particular Powerland currency, we have taken risks and had adrenaline-arousing adventures on the way. When we are in Powerland and doing Powerland-related activities, we are secreting a lot of adrenaline. Adrenaline is the ultimate reward in Powerland. All of us in Powerland are addicted to adrenaline (excitement junkies). We also may be addicted to other chemicals that get secreted in our body when we are enraged, as we often can be when someone threatens us on our way up. So, we look for situations that will get this adrenaline and those rage-chemicals going again. The rage chemicals include cortisol, which is a stress-reducing hormone, endorphins which are feel-good and feel-no-pain hormones, and dopamine, a hormone that makes it a pleasure to be rageful and allows us to focus on the object of our rage (Nathanson, 1992, pp 101-106).

We seek more and bigger challenges. We pick fights. We experiment with other people's lives. We constantly raise the bar.

When we are at the top, except for when someone wants to unseat us, there is really nowhere else to go, so there is some feeling of disappointment, perhaps boredom accompanied by restlessness for more action of the kind that brought us to the top or enabled us to get the job done. When we are at the top, we say, "Hey! What's next? I'm just sittin' around on my hands! What's that going to accomplish?! What the hell are we gonna do? Sit around, hold hands, and sing 'Kumbaya'?" (These are the actual words of an alpha that Marty knew!)

How could someone who grew up in this place ever learn to love? For years, although our culture has proclaimed and celebrated the value of the common man and membership in voluntary communities, in fact, the highest reward and acclaim have gone to those who went for the top. We have believed that the top of the Powerland mountain is the *best* place to be, that only the *real* winners make it to here. That is true; people who "win" at all costs have won *something*. Unfortunately, no one has told us the price of triumph. When we arrive at this cold, barren place, alone in victory, we have suffered the greatest loss anyone can suffer: we are without love.

We have sacrificed love on the altar of power. The fuel in Powerland is adrenaline, but we buy our adrenaline at a very high cost, and that is our family and other intimate relationships. Our castle on the hill in Powerland is cold and empty. It sucks. There can be no love in Powerland. If you want to spend the rest of your life in Powerland with its smile-less wealth, bitter sycophants, empty lifeless sex, don't bother reading any further. You will live and die alone, well served, but unloved. However, if you need help finding your way out of the trap of loveless Powerland, read on. Both of the authors have lived and triumphed in Powerland. And we have left it. If you want love, read on.

Understand: Loveland and Powerland are separate realities, separate cultures with separate languages. Unfortunately in America, both languages are called "English." Powerland and Loveland have the same vocabulary and grammar. Nonetheless, tone, facial expression and context produce opposite meanings for the same sentence. For example, in Loveland, "I will take care of you," equals a commitment to caring for and helping the other. In Powerland, the same sentence, "I will take care of you," conveys either murderous menace and/or a corrupt payoff for services rendered. For guidance in Loveland, read this book. Conversely, the best guidebook for success in Powerland is Robert Greene's *Forty-Eight Laws of Power* (2000).

Loveland

Loveland is warm and safe. It is a state of mind in which our aspirations for greatness do not smother our longing for happiness. In Loveland, we are allowed to be strong and cared for, to be a leader and imperfect, to be loved and to love. In Loveland, we don't see how big someone's home is, only how comfortable and inviting it is. In Loveland, we can freely and continuously connect. In Loveland, both love and achievement are valued. In Loveland, achievement of each of its citizens occurs within a web of relationships, in which there is loving support for individual achievement. In a land like this, you don't have to kick someone out of the way to keep climbing. Individual achievement occurs while we are mindful and respectful of others within the web; it occurs in a context of gratitude for the support of others.

In Loveland, there is an "all-are-winners" philosophy, a win-win philosophy. Each person's contribution to the web of relationship and to the total functioning of the group is appreciated, as well as her or his individual accomplishments.

In Loveland, we are not afraid to have others take us by the hand. We no longer look for their weapons. Instead, we see their help for what it really is, not what they are trying to get from us. We stop projecting our paranoia onto others. Loveland is a *land without malice.* It is not a land in which anyone will, on purpose, inflict harm on others for any reason, no matter how much they are hurting us. People may cause harm to us through ignorance, incompetence or neglect, but not through intentionally wanting to hurt us. Hurt is never inflicted, even when someone really feels like hurting others who are sources of pain, or hurting others just because they can be hurt, or because hurting has entertainment value. The absence of malice is a primary rule in, and definition of Loveland, one of its very highest values. Malice is the deliberate hurting of others, through action or through lack of action.

In Loveland, the highest value is connection, staying connected in a continuous way. This doesn't mean that people don't go off and do their own thing; there is respect for that. They just do their own thing in a way that is respectful to everyone else, and often with everyone else's support. The essence, the point of life in Loveland, is to create and maintain a connective environment for all of the people who live there and if something interferes with that, to fix it quickly, in a way that restores the connective environment.

This connective environment doesn't apply only to you and your partner because Loveland partnerships depend on the web of their other connections in Loveland, such as their extended families, friends, and community. This dependence on and connection with others in Loveland supports and enriches the partner relationship. Likewise, the partner relationship gives back to the community.

There are a lot of service-oriented community organizations in Loveland, and the people in these organizations work together cooperatively, often rotating leadership. Leading is not about being powerful. Leading is about giving one's skills and power in a loving way, for the purpose of getting the job done and serving the community.

It's not that in Loveland people are altruistic all the time. Rather, people are always feeling their way, in a caring and honest demeanor toward one another, to make sure that there is a proper balance between taking care of one's self and taking care of others in the relationship. Each person in Loveland needs to be quietly in touch with his or her own needs, wants, and desires, as well as listening to, hearing and, when appropriate, attending to the needs, wants and desires of others. There is continuous attention to balancing *everyone's* needs.

People are separate human beings, with their own sets of needs, desires and wishes and with different perspectives and experiences. When all goes well, this makes for a rich and interesting variety, like an elaborate meal with dishes from many exotic places, or a car show with lots of unique and expensive imports and classics. Others' separateness and differences in perspective and experience are as worthy of respect as our own.

More authentic emotions of joy and excitement are experienced in Loveland. The feeling of excitement in our bodies follows the pattern of the curve of sexual excitement. It starts small and slow, mounts to a peak, and then subsides. Joy, on the other hand, starts big and tends to diminish. While neither of these emotions is a constantly enduring state, both excitement and joy can be repeated; and they are, if enough time is spent in Loveland. When we are in Loveland and experiencing these feelings, the disappointments, interruptions and inconveniences that inevitably occur in relationships can be particularly disturbing.

In our imaginary map, Loveland is a much flatter place than Powerland. Powerland is a big rock mountain with swamps in the lowlands and crowded dwellings built up the side of the lower slope. On the upper slope are McMansions and gated communities hidden by exotic trees. The highest part of the upper slope leads to the barren caldera (the hole on top of the volcano) where the "maximum leader" lurks. He has a view of all the homes below him. He needs it; he's paranoid about people climbing up the slope and usurping his position. Loveland is greener, and has hills and dales, but no mountains. It is more like a beautiful golf course. The topography is variable but pleasant.

Pat remembers one morning when she stepped out her door and saw a beautiful spider web, embedded with rainbow-colored drops of dew sparkling in the sun. A soft breeze blew, and each drop trembled and changed its relationship with every other drop. Loveland is like this, with each person being a delicate sparkly drop of dew in the web. If you touch one drop of dew, the other drops also tremble. Everyone knows that a change in one affects the whole web, and so they become mindful of their own thoughts, words, and actions. If they miss something, or unintentionally do something that negatively effects someone else, they listen to hear from others about the effect they are having on the web. No one is bitten by the spider during life. Death however comes to everyone, in Loveland and Powerland.

Now, if you are an alpha, *Loveland may sound like a boring place to you,* perhaps like *Pleasantville* in the movie with the same name. But wait! Even if you haven't been successful in intimate relationships, you no doubt have fallen in love. Do you remember how that felt? There was a feeling of peacefulness in your heart, an "all's right with the world" feeling. While you also performed in other areas of your life, in your relationship there was a feeling that you didn't have to strive, that it was all right to be you. Your heart felt full. Do you ever miss that? Do you ever want to feel it again? Do you want to feel it more? "Those feelings aren't real," you may reply.

Those *feelings* are *real*, but they may not be *based on reality*. When we first fall in love, those feelings are often based on whom we *imagine* our partner to be, often on an idealized image of our partner. But the feelings of joy, of not being so alone in the world any more, and of being cared about are real. In Loveland, not only are those feelings commonplace, but they are real and sustained and only get fuller and deeper as we stay connected with our partner and other members of Loveland. Not only that, they are not based on some fairy-tale version we have of our partner; they are based on an authentic relationship with a real person, whom we are getting to know better and better. So the feelings last and deepen.

Two Lands: Your Choice

Powerland and Loveland are two separate worlds, each with its attendant world-view, priorities, attitudes, associated goals and behaviors. If you are an alpha, they are each places inside you. Your essential choice in an intimate relationship is to either live in your Loveland world 100% or live in Powerland, pretending to be in Loveland. Visitors to Loveland are tourists, pirates, or some combination of both. Tourists buy the natives' goods as cheaply as possible; pirates steal them. Both are exploitive.

In Powerland, evil is real, active and pervasive, and it is at the core of one's identity. Many players in Powerland don't think of themselves as evil. However, evil by definition is the ongoing willingness to cause harm in order to advance one's own perceived interest. In Loveland, any harm that occurs is caused by neglect, incompetence, or ignorance, not an active desire to exploit, dominate, and hurt others.

As you choose the land in which you want to live, we promise you that choosing Loveland is not the equivalent of being neutered. Loveland needs good strong alphas. You just need to learn about your liabilities and how to manage them.

It Takes All Kinds. Alphas and Betas Make a Village.

Betas are born into Loveland. There are roles for alphas in Loveland. There are several ways of being alpha.

For illustrative purposes, let's go back to the old frontier towns in the Western United States, in their early days of settlement. Mostly there were just men in these towns, with perhaps the exception of the local madam and her employees. The men in these western towns were real Powerland players; the toughest and smartest and quickest-draw was at the top of the power heap. All the early comers were alphas.

The alphas got lonely. Some decided to import some nice woman to marry. Then the new schoolmarm arrived. Some of these scrubby guys cleaned up and used their alpha skills to become Wyatt Earps. They turned into trusted alpha sheepdogs for the community.

What is a sheepdog? A sheepdog is a dog fast enough and aggressive enough to fight off predators. Sheepdogs do not eat sheep; they may, however, nip their heels, bark and do other annoying things to lead them around. Sheepdogs like to protect the workers, both alphas and betas, from the criminals, politicals and other self-serving predators. Some of the sheepdogs turn into good politicians; they may become mayors, and rule the town in ways that address the needs of the whole community. To them, governing is a way to be a good sheepdog. However, there are other types, one being the "lone wolf" alpha: the bounty hunter who goes out to find the outlaw, or the cattle driver who spends long days, alone, in the saddle, but still doing a necessary job. There are also predators who take advantage of the weak; they like to eat (exploit, take advantage of) whomever they can. Some alphas turn into outlaws. They rob the stagecoach. The loan sharks, pimps, criminals and some criminally entrepreneurial types are the predator type of alpha. Some politicians may masquerade as Wyatt Earp alphas, while taking bribes from the outlaws or the land-grabbers. They are also the predators of the community.

Alphas have affiliative instincts. If you didn't have them you wouldn't be reading this book. Loveland needs Wyatt Earps. It needs sheepdogs because the world can be, from time to time, a dangerous place. People need protecting. Loveland can integrate a large percentage of alphas. If you, as an alpha, were raised in a fairly loving culture, you can generally color between the lines and know how to live here. Sheepdogs and sheriffs think of themselves as good lovers because they protect everyone, but they still have some alpha-killer instincts. Examples of Wyatt Earp types are soldiers, firefighters, and police people who maintain their personal integrity. Alphas enjoy their Wyatt Earp role, as long as they don't feel threatened.

Roll time forward a hundred years. You can still see the alphas in the workplace and the community. These alphas fall into two or three categories; the third category is comprised more of betas, but it still has some alphas.

The Do-Dogs: Alpha and Beta

There are alpha and beta Do-Dogs. These alphas are sheepdogs of the human species. They are the Wyatt Earps of our western town. These are the guys who organize the barn-raising for the neighbor whose barn burned down. In today's community, they are present in the workplace, or in volunteer organizations, to get the job done. They are the hero firefighters and police and nurses. They are good soldiers. Their only purpose is to get the job done, and they will stare down (or worse) anyone who gets in the way.

Pat's nephew, Aaron, demonstrated this quality early on. Aaron's passion is cooking; his dream was to go to culinary school. No sissy, he also played football. At age sixteen, he had taken a job as a *sous-chef* in a very prestigious restaurant. His job was to make four or five specific entrees on the thirty-item menu when a customer ordered one of those. On his third night on the job, a party of seventeen ordered the same entrée, an entrée that was on Aaron's list. The assistant chef, upon hearing this, approached Aaron's cooking station with a worried look on his face. "What can I do to help?" asked the assistant chef. Aaron, already busy grabbing pans and ingredients, paused momentarily, looked the assistant chef directly in the eye, and said, "You can get out of my way." All seventeen dishes were delivered on time, deliciously cooked.

The Do-Dog alpha can sometimes be a "Freight Train" Do-Dog, who only looks at getting the job done, not at the human cost. In the example above, Aaron's priority was not to be considerate of the assistant chef's feelings; it was to get that food out.

There is the lone-wolf alpha Do-Dog. The bounty hunter or trapper of yesterday would be the housepainter or landscaper or plumber who has his own business and doesn't want any boss but himself; he just wants to be left alone to do his impeccable job. He may or may not be a family man, but as a friend, he would cover your back in a fight or rescue a lady in distress.

The shadow, the bad version of this lone wolf, is the outlaw. Today, this might be the drug dealer, the loan shark or, higher up, the crooked political lobbyist or Enron energy trader. You know, the guys who laughed about turning out the lights in southern California while gouging grandma because of Enron's approval of the ways they were gaming the system. They made bucks, and turned the people of southern California into clucks. Those bankers and Wall Street investors who bundled and sold bad mortgages and in that way are responsible for our economic debacle are another example of this kind of alpha outlaw.

The beta Do-Dogs are the hard workers, like the alpha Do-Dogs; however, they are also punctual, considerate, and respectful of authority; they go out of their way to be helpful, tend to take the blame upon themselves if something goes awry, and avoid confrontation if they can. They tend not to rise above middle management in corporations, as they lack the charisma and political skills of the Machiavellian alphas. They are the "good ol' Sams" who carry the organization's memories and have the necessary skills for getting things done that no one else has.

The Alpha Politicals

Universally, Politicals are alphas, with the rare exception of the highly competent and trusted beta, who may be pushed in a time of crisis into an unsought leadership role. Among the alpha Politicals, the good mayor of the old western town would be today's politician who really wants to serve the people, who believes in governance as a high calling; he could be the organizer of the homeless shelter. Then there are the outlaw alpha politicians. These shadow Politicals look like Do-Dogs and good politicians, but their priority is to look out for themselves. They are looking at getting the job done in a way that enhances themselves. Examples of this would be, again, the politician who takes bribes to promote special interest groups, or the guy at work who draws on quite a few people for advice on a project, delegates some of the work to subordinates, and then takes total credit for the job. For these shadow Politicals, life is a series of photo-ops.

The Love-Pups

This third group in the workplace can include alphas, but is generally comprised of beta males and women. Many of the Love-Pups want to get the job done, but *they want to do it in a culture of connection.* Their first priority is to build a team that works together well, all members participating, feeling good about their participation, *and* feeling good about the quality of their connection with others on the team. These are the people in the workplace who are always checking in with others to see how they are doing, how they are feeling and in addition, what they are accomplishing.

Most alpha Love-Pups are female. In any case, these people will use their alpha nature in the service of love and relationship. In time-priorities, these alphas focus on the team's working together so that the job will get done.

Connection is a Luxury

Do-Dogs and the Politicals have one thing in common. *What they have in common is that connection is secondary.* Whether the priority is to get the job done (as it is with Do-Dogs), or to serve the bigger community and/or to enhance themselves (like the shadow Politicals), connection will be sacrificed if necessary. *Connection is a luxury; people feeling good about themselves is a luxury, not an essential.* This attitude creates a big problem when they get home and engage in intimate relationships.

Whether in the western town, in today's workplace, or in our homes, certain things happen when alphas feel threatened. What happens when alphas feel threatened? Let's go back to our imaginary map. Loveland is right across the water from Powerland. For normal travel, there are bridges and ferries from Loveland to Powerland and back again. But we're more concerned with the Whoosh (Real, 2002): the alpha male's jet ride to his native land.

CHAPTER TWO

WHOOSH!
THE JET RIDE TO YOUR NATIVE LAND

In early adult life, alphas tend to live in Powerland and go to Loveland for entertainment and amusement. However, when an alpha moves to Loveland (often having succeeded in Powerland and therefore feeling good about himself), it is really easy to fly back to Powerland from Loveland. It is too easy. In Powerland, anytime you feel threatened, you respond *as if* your survival depends on eliminating the threat.

In the honeymoon stages of our intimate relationships, the primary unusual hormone that our body secretes is oxytocin. That is why we feel so wonderful when falling in love and while honeymooning; oxytocin gives us feelings of loving warmth, desire to always be with our partner, and delight in our partner. As people come in stages out of the honeymoon phase of their relationship, they discover a variety of ways in which they are not totally, naturally suited for each other; some of these are big ways. These difficulties are not easily or naturally solvable in fully satisfactory ways. Each partner will have at least one behavior, habit, attitude, belief and/or value that is very inconvenient for the other. There is always one part of each member of the couple that is so incompatible with the partner's needs, desires, and wishes as to be highly inconvenient. We feel pain in response to not getting our "ideal love."

These situations in intimate relationships can bring about unexpected feelings of threat. In Loveland, you can innocently be going about your business, happy as a clam, and then something happens. Your partner may surprise you with some disappointing behavior;

another person may innocently interrupt your happiness; or life, with its illnesses and tax audits and broken automobiles and other events, interrupts your happiness. Or differences between you and your partner "just don't work with who you are." You feel threatened, and reacting to that threat, you are automatically transported, by jet plane, back to Powerland. The trip can happen automatically, unconsciously and fast, even after you know more about it, which you will after reading this book.

We are referring to the jet ride to Powerland as initiated by the Oh Shit!! moment, which is caused by any hurt or threat. In his book, *How Can I Get Through to You?* (2002) Terrence Real called this moment the "Whoosh," which is a good name because it's as though there were a jet inside and outside your body that delivers you to Powerland in a whoosh, a split second. The mechanism, the trigger for that jet plane ride back to Powerland, is any kind of discomfort that will occur in a loving relationship.

The Oh Shit! moment is a sudden fall from grace. One moment we feel okay; the next moment, we're in Hell. What is Hell? Physiologically and emotionally, it is the emotion called shame. Our bodies collapse; our neck and shoulders cave in. Our spirit collapses along with our bodies, and we wish we could disappear. And then, *Whoosh,* we are back in Powerland, and we feel empowered to survive, no matter what the odds. When we whoosh back to Powerland, our natural response is a Power response: defending, attacking, tricking, cajoling, charming, shaming back, intimidating. There are many tools. We don't just want to hurt our partner back for hurting us; we also want to fix her or him so that he or she doesn't hurt us again. We want to get our partner to do what we want, so that she or he is not an inconvenience to us anymore.

The problem is, our partner is a separate human being with his or her own needs, desires, and wishes and with different perspectives, values, and experiences. In Loveland, their differences are as worthy of respect as our own. In Powerland, their differences take second or third or even fourth place to our own needs, desires and wishes, especially when we are hurting because we have been thwarted.

When we are hurting, and Whoosh back to Powerland, it feels as if our partner may be purposefully trying to hurt us. In Loveland, even when we fear purposeful harm (malice), both alphas and betas refuse to inflict pain in return. We maintain safety by soothing ourselves (See Chapter Fifteen). In Powerland, however, we want to hurt them back because hurt is a form of control, the way we demonstrate our superiority. This is the Whoosh moment, the Oh Shit! moment. If this happens over and over again, then we have begun to use our Powerland tools to aggressively initiate the extortion of extra goods from our "loved ones." (Of course, this cannot happen unless our partners allow it.) It is a way that we expropriate resources (time, sex, accommodation to our wishes-you name it) that would otherwise be unavailable to us without such intimidation. In a partnership, these unavailable resources might be love in the way that we want and expect it: ways that our partner doesn't have that go against their nature to give us. This attempt to hurt the other and demonstrate our superiority by controlling their giving us what we want is called *extortion*. In Powerland, one tenet is that he whose extortions are allowed to persist "wins." For those readers who are being extorted by alpha males, Terrence Real's book *The New Rules of Marriage* (2007) has excellent advice for how to prevent, deal with, and/or fix extortions.

The nature of alpha people makes it difficult for them to live in Loveland, even if they want to. This is because life is inherently difficult, and all kinds of things go awry, again and again. So, alpha people often end up in Powerland again and again. This happens because they treat unanticipated negative emotions as something to conquer. We want to get rid of negative emotions and perhaps even the other person. We want to get rid of our negative emotions by doing something to, with, or about the other person so that what they are doing will not be problematic for us. If we can only get those sons of bitches to see it our way and cooperate with us so we can get what we want we can feel better again. Inconveniences to us are treated as if they were problems to be solved. The solution, therefore, is to *get the other person to change*, or to extract solutions from her/him. If necessary, force of some kind is used, even if it is charming personal force, sometimes called charisma.

For an alpha person, the response to a negative emotion is to be tempted to harm either the cause of the negative emotion, or whoever happens to be handy, because we need a "tension release."

Negative Emotions

An alpha experiences any discomfort as a threat to his survival. All negative surprises lead to the Oh Shit! moment. The first emotion that gets triggered, deep down inside by the Oh Shit! moment, is shame. Nature designed all humans to have shame (Nathanson, 1992, p. 211). Shame enables us to be reprogrammed by our culture. Shame feels so bad that, for betas, they regularly accept further instruction. For alphas also, the moment of shame is a "reset" moment; it is the most teachable moment for alphas. We are innately programmed to stop, collapse, and open up to new information from our spouse, our family, teachers, and other parts of ourselves. Unfortunately, when we let the Powerland part of ourselves be our counselor, we get the wrong conclusion, the wrong re-teaching. However, under the right circumstances, in our moments of shame, if we can hold ourselves there, we are most open to learning really useful things. On the other hand, if another alpha is acting out of malice and shaming us in an effort to make himself feel good and/or exploit or manipulate us, that shame, which is not designed for re-learning or reset, is called "toxic shame."

When we feel shame, we want to go bury ourselves somewhere. And shame is not *just* a feeling. When we experience that emotion, there is a reduction of some body biochemicals, namely serotonin, norepinephrine, dopamine, and endorphins. These are chemicals that work in our bodies to keep us thinking sharply, focused, functioning well mentally, and feeling good emotionally. Endorphins and oxytocin are secreted in high levels in the body when we fall in love and at a more moderate level when we manage to stay in love in a long-term partnership. They are "feel good" hormones in the body. The Oh Shit! moment turns all that good juice off.

Exercise:
Remember some time, perhaps in your childhood, when you felt really ashamed. See how you looked; remember how you felt.

Write about any feelings you had about wanting to hurt either the person by whom you felt shamed or someone else.

Write about any "lashing out" behaviors in which you participated.

How long did your feelings and associated behaviors last? How did you get over it?

When we experience shame and stay open, while learning from our partner about the impact of our words and behavior and what we might say and do differently, our spirits are lifted. The levels of endorphins, oxytocin, and other "feel good chemicals" increase in our body. Anger will get us the same "fix" because, when we experience anger, there is an increase in the levels of the same body chemicals, with the exception of serotonin. The increase in these biochemicals causes us to be "red hot," energized, and pain tolerant. It is no wonder that when we experience shame, we quickly flip to anger and rage. It feels a lot better than shame. We feel much more in control, at least of others who have, by their behavior, been part of an incident to which we have responded by initially feeling ashamed.

However, there is a way in which we are seriously out of control of our own behavior. Our anger and rage can be homicidal. You may say, "Oh, no. I'm not really homicidal. I just need to deal." But our words in this state echo our deep feelings. We say things like "I'm gonna kill that son of a bitch." or "They'll be sorry they messed with me." We probably will not go out and kill someone, though it is during the storms of these anger-related biochemicals that some violent crimes are committed. Our homicide is more likely to be "killing someone off" by defaming her or his character, calling names or blaming them for our bad temper. We can certainly do death to a relationship during these periods, or at a later, more auspicious time. Anger is a dangerous emotion because it tends to generate increasing intensity and it can go off the chart; there is no top to anger (Nathanson, 1992, pp. 101-106).

"I really don't have any control over this," you might say. You might say, "It's just who I am." The truth is, you do have control.

If you are really honest with yourself, there is a split second, and it really is just a split second before or after you Whoosh off to Powerland, when you have a choice to stay in Loveland or to return to Loveland if you have momentarily abandoned it. For the first 180 seconds that you are back in Powerland, you can still redeem yourself. However, for every second that goes by, you are less likely to.

If you have let the golden three minutes go by, put duct tape over your lips, sackcloth over your head, and hide until you are fit for human consumption. If your partner wisely calls a crisis, mumble loudly through the duct tape and the sackcloth identifying a time you will be able to speak lovingly again and explore this incident together. Don't worry. We will tell you more about what constitutes a crisis (Chapter Seven) and how and when to use duct tape later in the book (Chapter Nine).

We know you can do this. You exercise that control at work with your boss and/or your customers when you have to. If you didn't know how, you wouldn't have made it as far as you already have in your life. We love Terrence Real's (2007) response to people who say that they do not have control:

> Imagine that a state trooper stopped you for speeding on your way to the most important business meeting of your life. Your whole career, thousands and thousands of dollars, rests on this deal. Now this officer is a real SOB; he's deliberately rude and keeps you waiting forever just out of spite. Every muscle and nerve in your body is dying to tear into him. But do you think that you would? Of course not! The consequences would be too great. You know what we call that? Controlling your anger. Guess what? If you can do it *there*, you can do it *here*. Those very sick people who truly cannot control themselves can't control themselves anywhere. No one *selectively* loses control. (p. 110)

The key is that you do have control. So, if you make a commitment to learning to stay in Loveland, you have the power to do that. Or you can fail yourself and become an end-stage, bitter rage-rat. Those are the choices. This book will teach you how to make and implement a commitment that will enable you to stay in Loveland.

First, we must tell you about another piece of the problem that is a challenge to an alpha male who wants to live in Loveland.

CHAPTER THREE

DEAF, DUMB AND BLIND.

Did you ever hear the song about the pinball wizard (The Who, *Tommy*, Pinball Wizard, 1969)? Remember him? He was the guy who was "deaf, dumb and blind, but he sure played a mean pinball!" Although we are Powerland wizards, compared to women, even most alpha women, alpha men start their adult lives deaf, dumb and blind in the world of emotions and relationships. By the time they reach adulthood, guys are biologically wired differently from women. We don't know for sure the effect of the violent training of males that we referred to earlier, or whether males are wired this way when they are born. However, by the time they are attempting intimate relationships, alpha men are wired to be leaders and hunters and therefore less emotional, less expressive, more pain tolerant (physical and emotional), and more monofocused than women.

Neuroscience research suggests that men have a lot of "inhibitory wires" from the prefrontal lobes of their brains, the thinking areas, down to the emotional centers of their brains. What that means is that you are likely to register thoughts and events without noticing your feelings as much as a woman would in the same circumstance. Also, there are fewer connections from these emotional centers up to the thinking centers of the brain. Therefore we can look our prey or our enemies in the eye without flinching, freezing or fleeing. Consequently, even when we *do* feel something, it doesn't register in the thinking areas of our brains in the ways that it does in a woman's brain. Further, most women have a lot more neural connections from the emotional centers in their brains to the speech centers of their brains than men do. So, when men *do* feel something, we have a much harder time finding a way to express it in words. We certainly have a harder time than most women, who have many more neurological connections from the emotional centers of their brains to the speech centers of their brains.

This difference in neurological wiring makes men better at suppressing emotions, including the emotion of fear. It leaves us often clueless as to what is happening emotionally to us or to others, and worse yet, speechless when we do begin to recognize emotions (our own or those of others). The difference in neurological wiring also leaves us uncomprehending when someone else speaks to us about emotions, their own or others. Isn't it disgusting sometimes when we need to talk with a woman about feelings and she goes on and on so articulately about her feelings and all their nuances, and we struggle just to figure out what it *is* that we are feeling, and we can't even *begin* to put it in words? Finally, with all her talk, she just boggles us, and once we're boggled, the words coming out of her mouth might as well be a foreign language! It's not only disgusting, but humiliating, because as an alpha, we don't want to be bested at anything, including talking about feelings; and here we are in the situation where our neurological wiring handicaps us and makes us look like idiots, even to ourselves! In summary, while alpha men are wired well for hunting and leading, by the time they reach adulthood, they are wired poorly for knowing and communicating about emotion in relationship.

Alphas "tend to have sharp minds, in neurological terms, optimal or advanced cognitive abilities" (Ludeman and Erlandson, 2006, p. 202). These sharpened abilities are located in the frontal cortex of the alpha brain. When complex decision-making is required in ambiguous situations, the alpha is on his best turf. However, our human emotions evolved for, among other things, short-circuiting the cortex in emergencies so that we can react instinctively to danger from our limbic system and brain stem. (Ludeman and Erlandson, 2006, p. 202) What this means is that when an alpha experiences strong emotions, he is likely to respond as his ancestors did on the savannah, as if his survival depends on either fighting, fleeing or freezing; and his thinking functions get overridden. It is often those very thinking functions we need when we feel strong emotions that are bound to come in intimate relationships, when we feel *as if* our survival is being threatened.

In the world of relationship, alphas are, prior to training, beginners. Training strengthens alpha neurological wiring so that we can know what we feel and how to talk about it. That is 50% of the problem.

Another 45% of this deaf, dumb and blind problem comes from the peer training that we talked about earlier. We were either born an alpha, in which case our alpha traits were reinforced, or we were trained to act like an alpha. Those of us who are over 35 were probably trained to "put down" skills that were and are considered "girl things," including feelings and talking about feelings. The poor beta male, for whom these skills occur more naturally, is often called "Pussy," or told to "act like a man." That's how his training begins. Women, on the other hand, are trained from birth to be attentive to the feelings of others around them as well as their own feelings and to talk about them, at length.

The remaining 5% of this problem in males is a result of parental examples and beliefs. You may be fortunate enough to have a father who treats the women in his life respectfully and who has learned well enough how not to fly to Powerland during times of partnership difficulties. On the other hand, you may have a father who has shown you by example that you must keep a woman in line or show her who wears the pants. If you did, that training also contributes to the deaf-dumb-and-blind situation.

That is the bad news. The good news is that neurological links can be grown with practice and frequent activation. The brain has an enormous ability to form new connections among brain cells. Recent research has indicated that some new brain cells become available during adult life. You might have been very uncoordinated, short on the neurological links that would make you a good golfer or fly caster when you first took up these skills. Now these skills may seem like second nature to you after thousands of hours of practice. The brain has lifelong plasticity. You know this because, at work, you haven't killed your boss or a difficult customer; you have taken charge of those feelings. Likewise in your intimate relationship, your lifelong training in Powerland responses can be turned off and not acted on. First of all, don't be an asshole (See how in Part II). Second, you must practice Loveland habits (also in Part II). Persistently acting ***as if*** we are natural citizens of Loveland can actually grow neuronal connections in the brain! The "fake-it-till-you-make-it" strategy *can* literally produce changes in our brains!

Gene Cohen, M.D., Ph.D., professor of health-care sciences and psychiatry and founding chief of the Center on Aging at the National Institute of Mental Health, reports new findings that brain plasticity does not decline with age (2005). Rather, it can actually increase as people get older. "Not only does the brain retain its capacity to form new memories, which entails making new connections between brain cells, but it can grow entirely new brain cells—a stunning finding filled with potential." Also, older brains "can process information in a dramatically different way than younger brains" (Cohen, 2005, p. *xv*). One solace in learning these skills late is that we may actually have more neuronal plasticity than we did earlier in adult life when we were establishing ourselves. Scientific scuttlebutt also suggests that declining testosterone and rising oxytocin levels make it possible for alphas to be successfully affiliative later in life. Even Henry Fonda made his fourth marriage work.

You can learn to play a mean pinball. You can master a new set of rules. It's like learning from a skill book to play golf with a handicap or to fly fish, or ski, or play any other sport. You have some challenges. Do you know many alpha guys who know how to successfully build and run a business, who, in many other ways know how to be successful in the work world? Your answer is probably "Yes". On the other hand, how many alpha guys do you know who know how to successfully be in a good and loving partnership? Probably not many.

You just may be up to the challenge. After all, you are an alpha. You can do it! If you don't do it, your excuses are already listed in Chapter Nineteen.

CHAPTER FOUR

THE DRAMA TRIANGLE:

The Death Of Love Trap

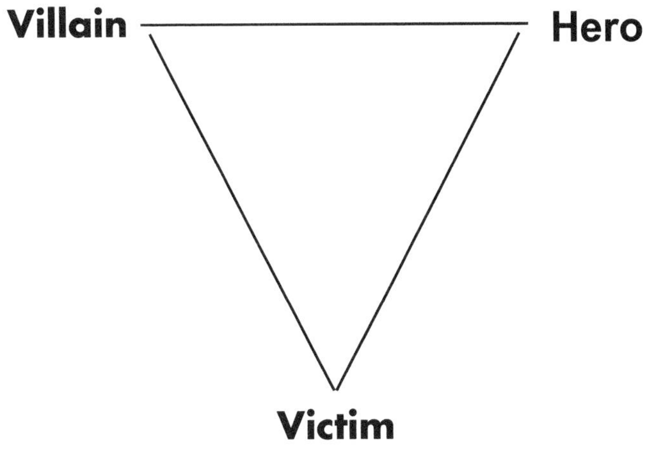

There's one more way in which you need to understand the problem, and that is to understand the drama triangle (Karpman, 1969; Polti, 1921). Drama is a form of connection. Love is a form of connection. If you are connected by love, there is no drama in the relationship. If you are connected by drama, the love connection is broken.

The problem arises when we are in Loveland, and we are in continuous connection. We might be feeling neutral, or we might be feeling joy or excitement. Then, the Oh Shit! moment occurs and we do or say something shameful. This moment may be triggered by a disappointment, an interruption, an inconvenience, or some irreconcilable difference. We disconnect, and the "Whoosh" to Powerland happens. We feel loathsome and unlovable. We wish we weren't here, or that our partner weren't here to see our loathsomeness.

We will be teaching you ways to prevent the "Whoosh" and ways to manage yourself when you do slip back into Powerland.

The problem grows if, upon our arrival in Powerland, we begin our Powerland ways, making even more severe our disconnection from our partner. Power plays drive drama. Participants in drama are still attached, but not connected in their hearts. You know those couples you see that make you think you *never* want to be married? Those couples are trapped in the Drama Triangle.

Drama is the essence of what we do in Powerland. Winning, losing, and rescuing are not about love. When we are on the drama triangle, we are still very much attached to each other. Now instead of being attached through love, we are attached through drama; the struggle to win, the struggle to not lose, the struggle to look good, and at worst, the struggle to get revenge and hurt the other person. Unfortunately, hopping on the drama triangle feels less vulnerable than working at getting back to authentic heartfelt connection. Staying with the truth of our heart and courageously and lovingly speaking our truth *feels* scary when we don't know how it's going to turn out. Will we fail, be humiliated, and want to die? No, we don't want to do that. It feels ***as if*** our survival depends on doing anything *but* becoming vulnerable.

We may feel fear, a fear that our partner doesn't care about us and will leave us, or that we are disappointing to them, or that in some way we will be irretrievably shamed, demonstrated to be worthless, humiliated. As anger has no top, fear has no bottom. We are capable, unless we do something to take care of ourselves and interrupt it, of falling deeper and deeper into a pit of fear. Anger and fear are biologically useful as signals that we need to do something to take care of ourselves. However, if we don't know how to read the signals, we don't know what to do. Or from past failures we know that what we usually do makes things worse. Our anger can be insurmountable and our fear can be undermining.

There are ways of managing anger and fear. Unless you have a program to follow when these emotions occur, you're not going to get anywhere. With anger, unless our life or the life of someone we love is at risk, we may need to take a deep breath or a few moments alone to calm ourselves. It is like the moment when you have hit your golf ball into the rough and you have to figure out how to successfully get it out, and you know that angrily breaking your club won't help, so you soothe yourself and get back to the game. With fear, we may need to take measures to address what we are afraid of, such as asking for help, reality testing to see if we really do need to be so frightened, or doing something to protect ourselves against that which we fear. Learning to calm yourself (See Chapter Fifteen) either when you are angry or fearful is useful and necessary. It is a step, but it is just a step. Alone, it is not enough. That is why you need more, and we are going to give it to you.

Further there is the emotion of sadness. Here's a scenario: We just lost our connection with our partner and ourselves. We lost our faith in ourselves and in the relationship; we lost our optimism about the future. With loss, the emotion that comes is sadness. While anger and fear are respectively topless and bottomless, the good news is that sadness is a finite emotion; it has a natural course. It tends to start with a high intensity and then to fall away if we let ourselves experience it.

The bad news is that as an alpha, not only are you not supposed to be afraid of anything, you *definitely* are not supposed to cry about it! Crying? That's what *girls* and *sissies* do! You may be interested in knowing that women perceive men who express their feelings, including sadness and fear, to be *very* sexy!

So instead of courageously feeling, acknowledging, and expressing these powerfully difficult feelings that are humiliating to display, we leap to Powerland, and onto the drama triangle. So with rage and anger, we exalt ourselves into the persecutor position. This is just what it sounds like. We disconnect from our partner and feel good about it, but lose all hope of reconnecting any time soon.

Does it mean that when we are disconnected, there's no attachment? No. We ain't that lucky; it ain't that clean. Because our relationship is a significant one, we are still attached, even when we are disconnected from a loving, trusting, heartful connection. In other words, there is a difference between *connection* and *attachment*. The attachment is still present, the other person is still important to us and us to them, but now we become assholes with each other unless it gets fixed in some mutually acceptable way.

There is contact, but it is full of drama. That's how people get on the drama triangle. They have a disconnect from Loveland, they go to Powerland and the form of connection in Powerland is drama. Ludeman and Erlandson have renamed the drama triangle the "alpha triangle" (p. 52) and we use their names for the positions on the triangle here. The drama triangle, or alpha triangle, has three positions, as we will explain.

1) Villain/Persecutor

This is the position we first choose after we are hurt and Whoosh into Powerland and jump on the Drama Triangle. This is what happens when we jump from shame to the anger state, wanting to transfer our shame and to make someone else feel bad instead of us. We feel like, "You hurt me, now *you're* gonna hurt!" It is from the villain position that we are likely to call names, assassinate the other's character, threaten to leave, or threaten (either overtly or covertly) to hurt someone if they don't do what we want. We make strong and powerful attempts to victimize the "cause" of our problem. We are often in the villain position if we find words coming out of our mouths such as:

"You better watch it or else!"

"Don't worry; I won't be around much longer."

"Bitch." (Or its variation, "Stupid Bitch!")

"Liar."

"You're Crazy!"

"How much do you want to regret this?"

"Now you've done it!"

And we must not forget Jackie Gleason's famous villain phrases:

"One of these days, Alice, POWEE! Right in the kisser!"
"To the moon, Alice, to the moon!"

We all laughed, but notice the threatened abuse, intimidation and, in one way or another, abandonment.

In the villain position, we can look down on others, shame and intimidate them, brush them off, secretly watch them because we don't trust them, and make them feel bad because we feel superior to them in our perspective on the problem.

2) Victim

In this position, our unhappiness is all someone else's fault. It is a "poor me" position. We act as if we are powerless to do anything to help ourselves and we send out either direct or indirect wishes to be rescued. We make victims of ourselves if we accept the villain's shaming, blaming or any other kind of overt or covert abuse. We are likely in the victim role if we find ourselves saying some version of the following:

"Poor me."

"I give him/her so much and he/she treats me like this."

"What can I do?" (This "What can I do?" is different from an honest, straight forward acceptance of some part of the other that we don't like. This version of "What can I do?" contains an element of giving up our own power, including power we might exert in the service of love.)

"You *make me* feel bad."

"It's your fault that I am always unhappy."

"I never get anything I want."

Frequent sighing.

Although alphas tend to experience the victim position internally, they are highly unlikely to show it, because the reigning alpha motto is "Die like a man!" However, their silent internal experience of the victim position drives them to bully even harder. The alpha male inner voice is saying something like, "You ain't gonna do this to *me*; I'm gonna hurt *you*!"

3) Hero/Rescuer

The hero rushes in to save the victim. Rescuing victims feels good. Heroes admire themselves. The hero reinforces the victim's pretense that he or she is incapable of taking care of themself. You know you are being a hero when you are:

Doing something for someone that they are capable of doing for themself.

Giving more than you want to give or have to give.

Giving up what you want in order to pacify the other person.

Sometimes when no crisis exists, you can cause a crisis by jumping into the hero role. Or when a crisis does come, instead of jumping into the villain role, you may jump into the hero role. Here's how it goes. If you are reading this book, you likely have spent a great deal of time helping others. You've been like our trusty sheepdog, protecting the people from malignant influences. If you are an alpha who likes to help, you most likely get on the drama triangle from the hero position. That is, you experience the disconnect as if your damsel is in distress and in a situation that needs to be fixed through your loving skills and advice.

She, on the other hand, thinks you are clueless. You may be, because if she thinks so, you probably are. That is because there's something about her that you are not picking up on or understanding. You are missing some clues from her; you are not seeing this as a problem that both of you are having. You may be the problem, or part of the problem may be about you as well as about your partner. At this point, neither of you understands the problem well enough to put it into a solvable form. You are flinging life preservers *of your choice* at her, and she is not up to being rescued by them, in part because they are of your choice, not hers. What is necessary is to reconnect. Otherwise, you can name yourself "Mr. Clueless Fixit." As an alpha, you really don't want to be inept in that way; the slower, but surer way to really help fix the problem is to reconnect, and listen, hard. With hard listening, you can get the "problem" described and defined in a mutually solvable form.

Here's a story of a couple on the Drama Triangle:

> Ben frequently loses his temper when Ellie goes on shopping binges that he feels they cannot afford. He Whooshes to Powerland and jumps on the Drama Triangle. He begins in the villain position. "You BITCH! One of these days I'm just gonna walk outa here and you'll be on your own. Then see how much you can afford!"
>
> Ellie responds from the victim position. She trickles some tears down her cheeks and begins to whine, "I work so hard around the house and you never appreciate me. Shopping takes the edge off all the loneliness that I feel living with you." Then she withdraws and silently watches soap operas on television for several days. "What is the use of my keeping the house if you're just going to treat me that way?" She is woeful victim, while also subtly being a covert villain.
>
> Ben starts to feel sorry for Ellie, perhaps a little guilty about his threats to Ellie and/or he just wants to restore the status quo without really being courageous enough to address the problem. He wants the house clean and his meals cooked again. He's shifting from villain to victim. He stops feeling bad as a victim by shifting to hero. So what does he do? He goes out and buys Ellie something even more expensive than she would have gotten herself and that they certainly can't afford. His cure? More hair of the dog that bit them! He presents it to Ellie with a "Hey, honey, I thought this would make you feel better." Now he has set himself up to be dumped out of hero position back into victim, because Ellie responds with, "You bastard! You think one more little something is going to make up for all the things you said to me?!" Ellie is now speaking from the villain position. Ben has now become victim. Defeated and depressed, he slumps, retreats to his workshop, grabs the hammer, and because he's tired of being the nail, pounds nails. He has now gone the full circle on the Drama Triangle.

Being on the Drama Triangle is definitely a form of attachment. The dramatic switches of role are driven by emotions that are stimulated by the power plays. Switching roles from villain to hero to victim is intrinsically unstable and is the essence of drama. The paradox is that you are simultaneously unstable and stuck. The stuck place is that you cannot get off the drama triangle by switching roles or spinning on the Drama Triangle faster, slower or differently. Every role, villain, hero or victim, is part of the drama.

The essence of the Drama Triangle is that no matter how much of the time you spend in one position, you are going to spin into the others. That's how couples get into really stupid cycles that are loathsome to watch, let alone take part in. However, because the Drama Triangle is a powerful form of attachment, people can twist together in the wind for decades. In this way, it can be a stable state; the drama just goes on and on. The drama may mutate over time, take on new forms, shapes, environments, player's personae, become even more subtle, or more dumb; but what's unchanging is that it keeps happening. The book and movie, *Who's Afraid of Virginia Wolfe*, is the classic characterization of chronic drama become fine art. The movie, *War of the Roses*, shows how if you spin faster and faster, and harder and harder, you can actually die of drama.

We disconnect, we unconsciously find ourselves on the Oh Shit! jet, and in Powerland, usually initially on the villain point of the drama triangle. And oh, how Powerland offers us a false embrace! The rules there are comfortable. We know how to be. We know what to do. We feel in control. We know how to win. All we have to do is to re-establish our power where once we felt shame. We can do this by getting power over the situation and over the other person. We can triumph!

There is a price. The price is loneliness and isolation, and the possibility that we will stay in Powerland and never get back to the good connection feeling we felt in Loveland. Inside, if we are lucky, we feel a niggling little voice, whispering to us that this doesn't feel good, that we are not behaving well. If we don't listen to that voice, we feel lonelier and lonelier, more and more disconnected from our partner and from Loveland. Loveland feels like a lush foreign oasis to which we will never return. If we do not immediately do something, we become more entrenched in Powerland; we begin to climb farther up that lonely rocky mountain. We find ourselves overworking, overplaying, overdrinking, cheating on our spouse, whatever, (any vice you like), to tune out our negative energy.

There is hope. There is something we can do. There is a way to jump in our little boat and row back to Loveland. There are ways to use our power in the service of love. In the following pages, we will show you the way out. If you want out, you must practice some proper procedures that make your Whoosh to Powerland happen less frequently. The guide is simple, but keeping to it is tough. Loveland calls us, and the horror of ending our life lonely in Powerland keeps us motivated. Love is your challenge. Get ready!

PART II: SKILLS FOR FIXING THE PROBLEMS

CHAPTER FIVE

BEGINNING BASICS FOR DEALING WITH PROBLEMS

What follows are basic understanding and tools that you will need to resolve problems in intimate relationships. There are only four kinds of problems in relationships, and we will discuss them later. First, you need to know the basics.

About Being a Volunteer

When a problem arises, the voices of Powerland shout at us. Power voices say things such as:

> "What the hell am I doing here?!"
>
> "If it weren't for you, my life would be better!"
>
> "My old life was better! *Any* life was better!"
>
> "Having to deal with *you* sucks!
>
> "Relationship! Who needs it? I am better off without it."

Remember, you unilaterally *volunteered* to be here. You signed up willingly. No one coerced you. Your partner, also a volunteer, is struggling right now too. You are both struggling with this problem and with these difficulties, because you volunteered to be in an intimate relationship. You made the choice to live in Loveland, whether you know how to live there or not. You made a choice that you hoped would insure that you don't die a lonely, isolated, miserable death. Your insurance against that miserable death is this loving partnership that just fell apart.

Reading this book, you are beginning an adventure, a challenging mission of never falling back on your Powerland ways and instead, learning the new and unfortunately initially awkward skills necessary for living in Loveland. You can console yourself with knowing that if you practice these skills, like practicing golf, skiing or fishing, you will feel more comfortable and less awkward.

This brings us to the next step, which is agreeing to always act in an absence of malice.

Absence of Malice

After you remind yourself that you are permanently a volunteer here, the next thing you must learn in a partnership is to proceed under all circumstances, foreseen or unforeseen, with *absence of malice*. If you are smart and lucky, you will have begun this practice before any problems arise, while you are still rosy-eyed and before you are knee-deep in shit. However, many alphas, especially alpha-alpha pairs don't arrive at a point of committing to acting without malice until they are already tired and beleaguered from hostile flights to Powerland. If this applies to you, you can call your relationship "The Fight Club." Many hurtful words have been said; it is harder and harder to get back to Loveland, and you increasingly miss being there. You know that the methods you have been using don't work; fighting this way will never work.

There must be a solid and sustained commitment to the absence of malice. Malice is actively, intentionally causing harm to others and/or passively allowing preventable harm to occur. Malice is a conscious decision. Do not proceed with problem solving until you have a commitment in place to not act with malice, no matter what. Before proceeding in any other way to deal with any difficult problem, you must make sure that you are in a place to keep that commitment.

What does this mean? Keeping a commitment to absence of malice means that we will do our absolute best to never use power plays against each other.

> We will never deliberately try to hurt the other, either with our words or with our actions.

We will not leave or threaten to leave.

We will not try to extort, through shaming, guilt, or force something that the other does not have to give, or cannot give, or does not willingly give.

We will not lie or twist the truth. Neither will we use truth as a bludgeon. Our truth is just that: our truth. Anything can be criticized from some point of view. We need to stick to claiming our preferences as preferences, not as criticism of our partner. For example, "I prefer to go to bed early" is very different from, "What's with this staying up until all hours of the night?!"

About Rage

Never rage at anyone you love. There are times we need to rage. If a child is raped, or someone we love dies, or we lose some part of our life that is dear to us, rage is one of several appropriate human responses. This rage is best expressed alone in a private and protected place, like the wilderness or our own room, where we can vent our rage as loudly as we need to. Alternatively, it is good to vent our rage with caring others who are not closely involved with our rage and who we have asked to bear witness to this expression of our agony.

If you rage at someone you love, someone who in the absence of malice has disappointed, interrupted, or inconvenienced you, that is a malicious form of self-indulgence, toxic to all present.

Seeing Your Partner in the Best Possible Light

The greatest service we can do anyone is to mirror their true heart.
Stephen Levine, *Embracing the Beloved*

Seeing our partner in the best, not the worst, possible light is closely related to absence of malice. In Powerland, the Powerland voices are front and center reporting for duty, if they haven't already taken charge. But that is not all that happens; *we begin to assume that our partner is also in Powerland and that they are thinking like we are.*

We are sure that our partner wants to hurt us or to get something from us in a sneaky way or betray us in any number of ways. We begin to assume the worst possible motivations for the particular behavior that has hurt or disappointed or inconvenienced us. Often, these are nothing more than projections of what *our* voice of power would *like* to do to them, or has done to someone else in the past.

Michael's ex-wife had cheated on him. He was so fearful and insecure that his current partner, Marcia, would do the same that he insisted on going everywhere with her. His unconscious goal was to isolate her from everyone, so that he could have all her time and attention for himself. Marcia had arranged with a neighbor to frame a beautiful family picture for Michael's birthday. In order for the gift to be ready for Michael's birthday, she needed to get the gift to the neighbor as quickly as possible. She told the neighbor that she would bring the picture over one afternoon while Michael was out of the house working on a project. To her chagrin, Michael returned home early. Marcia needed to either insist on going without Michael or not have the gift ready on time.

As predicted, when Marcia told Michael that she had to deliver something to the neighbor, Michael said that he would go with her. "I prefer to go alone," said Marcia. Michael pouted for the rest of the afternoon. After dinner, he lectured Marcia at length about how she was trying to isolate him from the neighbors.

A projection is when we literally project an intention or thought or feeling from our own mind onto another person and their mind. This often happens when we don't like the thought or feeling in our own mind, so we "throw it off" to someone else. We disown it. So, if *we* feel mean, we think *they* feel mean. Most alphas, however, don't mind knowing they want to hurt someone; in fact, they are often proud of it, because they have been taught that as part of "being a man" or a "tough woman."

In Marcia and Michael's story, Michael feared being out of control, including being out of control of when he would be alone. Therefore, he made intentional efforts to isolate Marcia from friends, relatives and neighbors, and to always accompany her so that he would not be alone. He projected this motivation of isolation onto Marcia, accusing her of doing just the same, that is, isolating him.

In Powerland, we are all paranoid. This is not like a very crazy paranoid schizophrenic; it is just part of the way our personality sees the world. Paranoids see others in terms of their possible harmfulness. Paranoia transforms our partner into a threat. This Powerland voice is whispering in our ear about how our partner is trying to hurt us and what might be their secret motivations. We wonder what secrets they might be keeping from us.

From a paranoid point of view, the issue is, "what is our partner up to?" What sneaky, nasty, betraying plan is afoot? What sugar-coated treachery is being offered in explanation?

In the absence of malice, all our partner has done to hurt us is to disappoint us, interrupt us, be different from us, or inconvenience us. In Powerland, we are warriors, trusting no one. The Powerland paranoid way of thinking and feeling projects its revengeful feelings onto the partner:

> I am innocent! You are the aggressor!
> I am wronged! You are the mean one!
> I am right! You are fucked up!
> I know you did that on purpose!
> Help! You are out to get me!
> I had no choice but to do that! You were going to do it to me!

In this process, we have disowned our own confused, painful feelings and turned them into perceived nasty motivations on our partner's part that explain and make seeming logic out of their pain-inducing acts.

> Josh was a light sleeper. He was also very jealous of his wife Elizabeth's relationship with her sister Anne. Before Elizabeth and Josh had married, Anne and Elizabeth would often talk on the phone early morning or late night. After Elizabeth married Josh, she asked Anne not to call before 9:00 a.m. or after 9:00 p.m. One morning, Anne, who worked as a nurse and was on her way to the early shift at the hospital, heard a weather report that a flash flood was headed to Josh and Elizabeth's vicinity. She awakened them at 6:30 a.m. to warn them of the flood. Josh became enraged. As Josh and Elizabeth talked about this later, Josh admitted that he thought that Anne and Elizabeth had planned the phone call in order to create a wedge in their marriage or just to irritate Josh because Anne didn't like him.

It is really important to recognize moments when we are seeing our partner through our paranoia and not in the best light. Part of the commitment to absence of malice is that, unless proven otherwise, we make the kindest possible interpretation of our partner's behavior. We refuse the voice of paranoia.

In case you are saying, "I'm not paranoid," you should know that everyone who is paranoid says that. The position to take is that your partner is innocent until proven otherwise. The effort that you must make is not to prove their guilt. Rather, you need to take a position of true curiosity about their process. What is really going on with them; what are they really thinking and feeling? Instead of ascribing the worst possible motivation to their behavior, we assume a stance of trusting their innocence, trusting absence of malice on their part.

However, sometimes we experience an Oh Shit! moment and a flight to Powerland because, despite their best intentions, our partner *has* catapulted into Powerland and its accompanying emotions and behaviors. If we recognize that we are both on the drama triangle, we stop marshaling *our* Powerland characters to combat *their*

Powerland characters. Instead, we engage our curiosity to wonder what might have triggered our well-intentioned loved one to have their own Oh Shit! propulsion to Powerland. We may need to firmly set limits in order to engage our caring curiosity about what is going on with them. DON'T FIGHT! Instead, shift to curiosity on how the hell we got here. Then proceed with setting mutual boundaries so that we can better avoid this in the future.

None of this implies making excuses for Powerland behavior or fooling ourself about our partner. Understanding is not excusing. Understanding gives us a handle to use in preventing repetitions of the disconnect. Connecting through curiosity about what happened feels better and is more promising than fighting. But it is not just about feeling better; the overall purpose of the connected curiosity is to prevent repetition of the disconnect.

> Doug and Marla had been visiting Doug's family in Paris for an extended five-week vacation. Doug had a history of becoming anxious when he and Marla were separated; he hated any separation. Because they were together for such a long stretch, he had suppressed his dread of a separation that was to occur during an upcoming visit with her sister that Marla had planned for the end of their trip. As the morning of Marla's departure arrived, Doug, his mother and his brother escorted Marla to the airport. Doug began yelling at his mother, telling her she never should have come. Heads began to turn towards Doug and his temper tantrum. Doug's brother was stunned, his mother frozen and ashamed. Internally, Marla felt embarrassed and experienced her own Oh Shit! moment. She was tempted to give Doug the same kind of treatment that he was dishing out. Instead, she took a deep breath, stiffened her spine, stepped between Doug and his mother, laid her hand on Doug's arm and said, "Honey, what is going on? You need to stop this RIGHT NOW because you are spilling toxins all over all of us. I'm very curious about what is going on inside of you. When you have cooled off, let's go talk."
>
> Doug took a deep breath and a stroll through the airport. When he had collected himself, he was able to tell Marla how much he hated it that they were going to be separated.

Does commitment to absence of malice mean that the Voice of Power turns off forever, becomes silent? Does it mean that we banish from our inner self the parts of us that want to hurt the other, or rage, or rave, or throw an intimidating anger fit when we feel shame? No such luck. The Voice of Power is in us for survival. It will not die. If we are an alpha, those parts will always live inside of us and they will often jump front and center, ready for instant action when we experience the Oh Shit! shame. So, we need to take charge. Take charge of what? We need to take charge of our inner Power Committee. What is that? This deserves a whole chapter.

CHAPTER SIX

THE INNER POWER COMMITTEE

Our brain deludes us into thinking that we are one person, the same all the time, 24-7. But stop and think about it. No way! Think about what you are like with someone you love and someone you are gentle with, like a child or a pet. Think about what you are like with your boss, or the person who is competing for your job, or some drunk at the bar. There is no way that the same part of us is dealing with each of these different people. So what are we?

Inside, each of us is a committee with many voices or centers. These centers have their own will, purpose and intention. For simplicity and so that you don't think that you are a nut case, we will call these centers committee members. This is *not* a multiple personality disorder! This is normal.

It is important to remember that each committee member would like to run the show, be in charge, and make all the important decisions. And each one, when he or she is active, thinks that he or she is all of you. Like a board room or a committee in the workplace, many strong members of the committee believe that *they* should be running the committee, that *their* voice is the most reasonable and that all the other guys should just go along. And if you let them, they will run the show. They will jump into the leader's seat in a New York minute!

So, who is in charge? Often, no one. We wobble, and are driven either by others' demands, if we see that they are stronger than we are, or by whatever committee member on our inner board grabs the leader's chair first.

Now, let's opt out of the boardroom for a minute and onto the ball field. A team really needs a coach, right? Do you have a coach? If not, you are the Bad News Bears. If we don't have a coach for these different inner voices, we must develop a very competent one. It is critical to have or develop a coach in order to keep our commitment to an absence of malice. The coach, like any good leader, must be aware of all the members on the team.

Who is the Coach and Why Do the Other Committee Members Listen to Him?

We humans are neurologically wired to have a coach; it is a matter of survival. We are structured this way so that we can neurologically construct a comprehensive map of the world (how things work, how one is supposed to behave in different situations, and what our values and beliefs are) and behave in a manner consistent with our comprehensive map of the world. The construction of our map of the world initially begins with the things we learn from our parents, extended family and peers, as well as from instruction from the community in which we are raised. Here is how it works neurologically:

We are genetically programmed and biologically structured so that we move around the world by using our own individually constructed map of the world. There is a portion of the brain, on the right side, in the preparietal area which, if intact, has a specific and unavoidable function. That function is to make a Value Map that will serve as our basis for making decisions as we move about our entire world. This map is a complete mapping of our world, with valuation in terms of survival, pain, and pleasure assigned to different spheres of life. From this area of the brain, we assign value and meaning to what we do. We are designed to have an overriding belief system about what is important, what's not, what's pleasurable and what's not, what is painful and what is not, what promotes our survival and what endangers it, what will make us look good in the eyes of our reference group, and what will cause shame. Without this preparietal area, we would be lost. It acts in ways that a sensible, slow and efficient computer acts, which is to look at the choices we must make in a given situation and to choose the best one, based on our Value Map of the world. (Best equals optimal: the most pleasure, the least pain now or later and the least risk to survival.)

The parietal areas of the brain, both on the right and left side, execute action in the world based on the values contained in our mapping in the right preparietal area. Our motor neurons are in the parietal area and these neurons choose and execute our voluntary activities. Massive practice (thousands of hours) of a skill set, such as firefighting or specific sports, makes it possible for us to perform well automatically with minimal data because of our powerful performance maps that let us know how to get the best result with the least risk and the least data necessary. Further practice of these optimal action sets, when successful, reinforce the Value Map, and make it more likely that the next similar situation will be dealt with according to that increasingly successful mapping of "reality." Reality is whatever picture you have that works over and over again.

The left and right prefrontal lobes have a list of no-no's, the Ten Commandments of things we have programmed into our brain that we will not do under any circumstance (Reiff, 2007). (We strongly suggest that you program Marty's Loveland Commandments, found on page 175, into your brain.) Depending upon our upbringing, we store in our prefrontal lobes additional judgments that we learned from parents, peers, and community, about what is right and wrong. The prefrontal areas look for things that shouldn't be done. They can shut down feelings, thoughts, and actions that go against its prohibitions.

Now follows a tricky part. Our verbal area, found in the left cerebral cortex of our brains, doesn't always understand the map of our right preparietal area. It doesn't always understand why our parietal lobes execute the voluntary action that they do. What it *does* know is how to make up a good story about why we have done what we do. We often act *as if* we willed the action prior to its happening; we confabulate about that. Some of that confabulation will be context-dependent. For example, why it is okay to tell a lie when talking with friends at the bar and not okay to do so at church (or vice versa!).

The left cerebral cortex and accompanying verbal area is the Public Relations Department of our brains. These verbal areas will tell us convincing stories of self-motivation, based on our personality structures; that is, if we are very logical people, our stories will be logical; if we are airy-fairy people, our stories will be airy-fairy. We are often convinced that the story is real as we tell it and many of us have no internal possibility of learning that we confabulated and why we actually fired off. This is why, after we have gotten more aware of ourselves, we have to take so much time to figure out what really went on and why we really responded to a certain situation the way we did. This is also why our recollection is often not congruent with our partner's recollection. (See Chapter Nine: Telling the Story.) Our left brains, relative to action initiated by the parietal areas, based on our maps in the right preparietal areas, are late to the scene and tell a story after the act. So, will you make up a story? Will I make up a story? You bet. And the best one we can.

We have all kinds of beliefs in our left cortex and all kinds of beliefs about our beliefs, and these beliefs may not be congruent with what is observed in our actions, either when we observe subjects in psychology experiments or in a natural setting. It is like when we believe that we are incapable of a certain behavior and someone captures us on a home video exhibiting that behavior. It is hard to believe.

A highly organized brain is congruent in all the brain centers that we mentioned above. The prefrontal lobes, those lobes that contain our list of judgments and no-no's, are congruent with our maps of the world contained in our preparietal areas and with our parietal areas that initiate our action in the world. The thinking and speaking part of our brain, the cerebral cortex, knows and can say clearly what is contained in our map of the world, what is congruent with our no-no list in our prefrontal lobes and why our parietal areas initiated the action they did. There is much less incongruent confabulation. Of course, we don't put it in words like that. The point is that there can be a high level of congruence between all those areas.

Higher brain organization is the congruent functioning of all our centers of will according to one map that is the responsibility of one center of will, composed of all the parts of the brain mentioned above. Those parts of the brain are the substrate for the center of will that we call the coach.

These various centers are like computer software that are also part of old value maps, if there are any. Without the overall mapping, any one of these "software programs" will take charge, as if it is the computer itself, or as if it is the coach, and not just a software program. What it cannot do is promote the greater good, according to the overall map, and according to the commandments of the land where you have committed to live as a good citizen. The coach that we spoke of above is a construct itself, a construct of the congruent functioning of all those brain parts. The coach is not only coach, but also a high priest, whose sacred role is to make sure that your needs get met. When our brains are working congruently, the coach makes sure that our needs get met in accordance with our commandments from other areas of our brain. Our brains are wired to have a coach and to be congruent, to have one belief system, with a clear hierarchy of values from which all actions are determined. When we are congruent we are at peace. When we are congruent we are maximally productive at whatever we have committed to value.

Examples of country founders who had congruency in their maps and acted accordingly are George Washington, Nelson Mandela, and Vaclav Havel. They had committed to congruent principles of a traditional kind, and stuck to them, despite pressure to become powerful in less ethical ways. George Washington, for example, was pressured to become king. Rather, he chose to proceed with the American democracy that his principles demanded. The men mentioned above acted congruently with their maps, even though hundreds of other founders went on to become tyrants. Those who became tyrants crossed the line and thereby destroyed any chance of staying sane, non-idiotic, and non-destructive. These include Idi Amin, Julius Ceasar, and the leaders of the French revolution who killed all the aristocrats (anyone who knew anything about governing) rather than re-cycling them.

These examples are clear-cut, black and white. There are examples of gray. One of these would be Vito Corleone in the movie *The Godfather*. Vito was basically a sheepdog alpha. He didn't want to be a bad guy. He came over from Italy to make a start in America, land of opportunity, with his family. He wanted to open an olive oil importing business. He found that America was full of bad guys who were out to control immigrants and their areas. He found himself in the swamps of Powerland and his family threatened either by others in the swamps or by bad guys who had crawled down from the caldera. So he pulled mud from the swamp and established a fortified enclave for his family. He never intentionally wanted to harm anyone unnecessarily. His decisions were always guided with his family in mind; he wanted to protect it.

By contrast, his son Michael stepped over the line, out of the gray sheepdog alpha role into clearly the bad-guy alpha role. Michael grew up wanting to survive by getting away from the family business. When he reluctantly returned, his primary business was personal survival, not protecting the family. Protecting the family and the community were secondary priorities. He was more self-centered, less family-centered. For example, for his own survival he had his brother killed. Vito was beloved. Michael was feared. His guiding question was "Who do I need to sacrifice in order to survive?" That's the difference between a somewhat more principled alpha sheepdog and one that steps over the line. For Nelson Mandela and George Washington taking care of the community was a priority over self-survival and self-aggrandizement. This was true even for Vito Corleone, clearly a criminal and over the line. But the fact that his first commitment was to family and community made him more like Mandela, whereas Michael was more like Idi Amin.

As an alpha, the map of the world in our preparietal area is a map of Powerland. That map tells us that we are born to lead, that we are special, that our first responsibility is to get what we want at all costs, that if someone isn't delivering what we want, we should get rid of them and keep looking, and all the other Powerland messages. Our Public Relations Department, our cerebral cortex and our associated verbal center, will give us, and our partner, a credible explanation for our tactics, reasons why we are unique, special, and deserve what we want. It also tells us why, if someone (like our partner) doesn't deliver, we should keep on looking for a different partner. Our prefrontal lobes, containing our judgments, are distorted if we listen to our own propaganda, spun out by our cerebral cortex, all our lives.

We allow different centers of will to be in charge at different times, depending on where we are and what we want. Sometimes the amygdala and the associated limbic system of our brain can take over higher functions of our brain. The amygdala is a primitive emotional center of our brain, the one that gives us only three choices: fighting, fleeing, and freezing. That's how we end up being the Bad News Bears, in need of a coach.

We have the capacity and the hard-wiring to construct a unifying, organizing coach who will allow us to live in Loveland and who will be in charge of other centers of will, members of our inner team. We have the capacity to re-structure the map of the world held in our right preparietal lobe. In today's world, with our economic, religious, and social structures changing, women are no longer economically dependent on men. Our churches and communities no longer encourage someone to stay in a relationship where they are consistently mistreated, or even to stay in relationships that are consistently without intimacy, even if they are treated well. We now have enough information from the behavioral sciences that we can carefully construct a new map of the world. John Gottman's research (Gottman, 1999) of over twenty years addresses research-proven behaviors that make marriages happy and those that don't. We also have the very good information in Terrence Real's (2007) teaching, and the skills we are sharing in this book. There is enough information about the best kind of relationship to have and what you are volunteering for if you want that relationship to be stable and happy. And every alpha, however narcissistic, will need to do this in order to reliably live in Loveland.

We must believe in something before we can take action of any kind that is coherent. A belief is the hierarchical value mapping in the right preparietal area, as supported by the commandments in the prefrontal area. When we have a world-view belief system built on Powerland rules, we must make a conscious decision to change our world-view map. Often, we are not ready to do this until we have failed often enough in our relationships and are desperate for a loving partnership because of our multiple failures. We lose faith in our old map but we have no clue about finding an alternative one, or that there even are solutions. The guidelines in this book are an alternative, based on sound research and years of clinical and life experience.

If we decide to make a conscious choice to follow the entire hierarchical value map of Loveland, this represents a total organismic change. If we decide to do this, there is one other thing that we should know. When we construct a new map in our preparietal lobe map room, the old maps don't go away. The brain retains all "previously successful" protocols in case they are needed. They hang underneath the new map. We can use these maps in situations where we need them, but not in Loveland. And because these maps never go away, in times of stress we are capable of regressive behavior. The more we use our new map, or exercise all the above-mentioned brain areas in ways congruent with our new map, the more synapses we grow and/or reprogram to support the new map. We become less likely to return to the old maps. And those old maps, the power maps, can be used in the service of love, to support love rather than to further enhance power. For example, Marty, who is dying of cancer, uses the power maps hanging underneath his Loveland map, to navigate in the world of financial investing. But rather than using the fruits of his labor to enhance his power or appearance of power in the world by buying a Ferrari, he uses the money he has successfully made to make sure that Leslie and his children and grandchildren will have financial resources when he is gone. This is Power in the service of love.

Our brain is hard-wired to have an overarching executive, a coach. The coach is a construct for the executive, the boss, if we choose to live in Loveland.
As coach, you must get to know your team members. They all have a role to play. As a coach, you gotta help them do their bit, right? Sometimes, a team member you didn't even know shows up and says, "Yep, I'm here!" As the coach, you need to figure them out, settle them down, and get them playing according to the team rules.

Sometimes, in the course of coaching your team, a softer, gentler guy may show up who knows how to do love. When this new team member shows up, the anti-love, anti-vulnerability crowd may get louder and increasingly insistent. This is because they get scared as you become increasingly successful in maintaining connection. They get scared into thinking that this guy will give away the ranch. As in any well-run team, the coach is responsible for listening to all the players, knowing their motivations, competencies and limitations, winning at the games he chooses to play and where he chooses to play them. The coach must not allow players who would be destructive to take over the leadership of the team.

Your highest value in your mapping is your "god." What we mean by that is that, for this "god," you will sacrifice all other values, even your own life. As an example, in an addiction, the substance or situation of choice is your "god." Some blues songs call this the Monkey, as in, "she was a Monkey Woman" to describe a woman with a cocaine habit. Whatever words we use, the meaning is clear; you are not in charge of your life; the habit or the desire is.

The Warriors

So, who are the guys on your inner committee who are going to give you problems? The defining characteristics of alphas are genetically determined both in our species and those studied animal species that have a social structure similar to ours, primarily other primates and various canine species. Why are we sure that alpha is a genetic trait? In identical twins who were raised apart, if the first twin is a narcissist, 80% of their identical twins are also narcissistic, despite differences in family and cultural environments, including different countries. This is a higher correlation than has been found in schizophrenia and possibly manic-depressive disorder, the two psychiatric disorders most strongly correlated with genetic predisposition. Since one can not be a narcissist without being an alpha, we believe this demonstrates the genetic nature of the alpha configuration (see Torgerson et al., 2000).

The primary defining characteristic is that of being born to lead. The other genetically based individuals are the betas who can learn to lead (especially males who are socialized by family and culture) but by nature they tend to shy away from competition, fighting, and conflict. Alphas find competition, fighting and conflict exciting; it gives them an adrenaline rush. The chronic overindulgence in these exciting activities can make an alpha an adrenaline junkie. Our code name for this trait is The Soldier. The beta, on the other hand, finds competition, fighting, and conflict anxiety-provoking and uncomfortable.

A second genetic trait present in some alphas and occasionally in betas is a highly developable talent for deception. We call this the Secret Agent. Alphas with a Secret Agent will implement plans that are never fully known by their associates. All the truth will never out. Machiavelli was one such alpha. In a recently published edition of his book, *The Prince* (1996), he so clearly, carefully, and extensively defined the necessity and benefits of deceptive leadership that his name has become attached to such strategies. Machiavelli wrote for princes. The best recent updated version of Machiavelli for the common man is Robert Greene's *Forty Eight Laws of Power* (2000). This book is an elegant, highly readable exposition on how to be a successful lifelong sneak and fraud at any level of power. The beta who has a Secret Agent tends to act in a solitary, sneaky, passive way, for example, the quiet bookkeeper who slowly embezzles a fortune from his employer.

A third genetic trait which has to date only been observed in alphas is a genetic tendency toward meanness and seeking pleasure in the pain of others (many feline species show this; for example, the cat playing with the mouse). Our code names for individuals with this alpha trait are Sadistic Bastard for guys, and Bitch from Hell for women. We have chosen acerbic code names for this third warrior because of their intrinsic nastiness. This nastiness is so horrifying and distasteful to the non-nasty that each gender has a long list of very ugly terms applied to individuals who have this trait and exercise it.

The dark side of being alpha interferes with loving relationships. The Secret Agent and the Sadistic Bastard/Bitch from Hell intrinsically destroy the capacity to maintain loving connection. For maintaining absence of malice, the coach needs to make sure that the dark side of the alpha does not show up in your relationships. If the Secret Agent and the Sadistic Bastard/Bitch From Hell are present they must be excluded from relationship at all times.

We will unpack these genetic types now and then we will discuss the subtleties of the specific roles and strategies that each of these various types can manifest in their behavior.

Warrior I: The Soldier

(The General and his Private, the Godfather and his Thug, the Dictator and his Foot Soldier)

Every alpha male and female has this warrior on his squad. This one is universal and is part of what defines us as alpha. When it is good, it protects and provides, like the sheepdog. When it is bad, it is the bullying thug part of us. This is the part that wants to kill, maim or destroy whatever or whoever has shamed us, even when it is the partner we love. We want to eliminate *anyone* when we perceive that they are obstructing or destroying our happiness. In Powerland, the motto is "When in doubt, rub it out." The Soldier can act without feeling. He can hurt, either in cold blood or in rage, if you let him. This persona has been active at those terrible times when your partner has been stunned and said some version of, "Who the hell are you? How can you treat me like this?"

Now usually the Soldier doesn't literally kill. In the business world, when we find that someone has tried to cheat us, has been deceptive, or wants our position, this is the part of us who knows how to "kill them off." We withdraw abruptly and often with no explanation for the one who is cheating. We offhandedly drop a few negative words to the boss about the one who is vying for our position.

Is the Soldier a *bad* part? No. Once we have the courage to face this part of ourselves, we can make good use of it, but *not ever* in an intimate relationship with a good person. This warrior can be used to protect the innocent. This is the lonely one who stayed up in the cold night without a showing campfire in the primitive tribe, alert for marauders. This is the soldier or partisan who fought Hitler in World War II. This is the firefighter and policeman or policewoman who died in the World Trade Center. If we should need someone to drive backwards out of a village in Iraq with a steady hand on the wheel, the Soldier is the one we want. This is because the world can unfortunately be a dangerous place and there is sometimes a need for him.

Alpha women have a Soldier too. Here is Pat's story of how her Soldier was useful:

> My daughter Ali won an expense-paid trip for two to New York City. I was honored when she asked me to be her traveling companion. It was late and we were tired as we stepped off the bus that had brought us from Newark Airport to the Port Authority bus terminal.
>
> My daughter was proud to be treating for the trip and had planned her expenses carefully. As a working single mother putting her through college, I was glad to go along with that plan. We had agreed to save money by taking the Newark bus to Port Authority and then, since the hour was late and 42nd Street still seedy, treating ourselves to a taxi from the bus terminal to the hotel. As we entered ground level of Port Authority with all of its late Friday-night New York characters, I warily began looking for porters and/or a taxi. To my relief, a man dressed in khaki pants and shirt, with some sort of official-looking patch on his shirt approached and asked if we would like help with our luggage. With relief I nodded and told him that we wanted a taxi. "Yes, yes," he

nodded as he quickly relieved us of our bags.

He walked briskly, about six paces ahead of us. This was in the early days of those shyster guys in New York who would dress in what appeared to be a uniform, grab your luggage and disappear. Word wasn't yet out about them, especially to two women just arriving from North Carolina. But something made me alert. I kept up with him and kept an eye on our luggage. He led us past a line of yellow cabs. "But," I said, "we want a cab." "Yes, yes," he said. "but in New York you must get the best deal. I will get you the best deal. Just follow me."

He led us into a parking lot. Sure enough, there were rows of vans with "Taxi" signs on top. He opened the third of four doors of one van and threw our luggage in, motioning for my daughter to get into that seat. He opened the second row seat for me. I got in, with a growing sense of uneasiness. "I'm going to get the driver. I'll be right back," he said. I was puzzled. Before I had time to think, the driver and another man were in the front seat. The "porter" was in the rear seat, behind Ali. My uneasiness increased: why would a porter join us in a cab ride? At that moment a tough-looking young woman rapped at the window. "I'm going on this one too!" she exclaimed as she joined our "porter" in the back seat.

Something was dreadfully wrong. Just as I thought of flinging the door open, grabbing Ali from the back seat and heading for the light and relative safety of 42nd Street, a large delivery truck drove into the lot, blocking access to the street. By this time our van was moving toward the dark street on the other side of the parking lot.

I first attempted to make contact with the driver, and his accomplice in the front seat, since they clearly were in charge. My inner coach sent forth a committee member, the interested, friendly, and engaging world traveler. My attempts to engage him by talking about my recent visit to his native country, Egypt, were met with silence.

We drove several more blocks. It was time to get down to business. "How much does this cab cost?" I asked. "Seventy five dollars per person" was the terse reply. This was a trip of about eight blocks, which at most would have cost seven to eight dollars in a legitimate taxi.

I contemplated the situation. My Soldier knew that we must not give forth any "scent" of being potential victims, of being afraid. "We're not paying that," I stated. "Then you will not get out of the cab," the driver replied. We were driving through an area that looked unsafe. I bided my time.

As we neared the hotel, I saw picket and police lines in front of our hotel and the adjoining building, the site of a strike. The picket line was between the sidewalk and street, preventing our access to the hotel. One member of my inner committee, the hopeful, peace-loving one, hoped the driver was bluffing and would let us out when we had passed the picket line. But my Soldier, ready for duty, reminded me of the mace that I carried in my purse. I slowly pulled it out, wrapping my hand around it to conceal it until I needed it. The car inched its way past the hotel and then past the adjoining building. It did not stop. We were almost to the red light at the end of the block. I heard the accomplice in the front seat say quietly to the driver, "Watch the light up ahead."

At this moment, I knew that these men had no intention of letting us out of the car. I pictured us beaten, robbed, or worse. Fiercely protective of my daughter and secondarily of me, the coach knew it was time for the Soldier on my committee to come front and center. Teeth bared, gripping the mace, a fierce voice came from my inner warrior, "You let us out of this *fucking* cab right this minute!"

For the first time, the accomplice in front turned to look at me. My warrior did not blink. "What have you got in your hand?" he asked. "Never you mind," I said, still not blinking, and then I reiterated my command. We locked eyes for a timeless moment while I mentally prepared to use the mace. The accomplice dropped his eyes. "Let her out of the car," he softly said to the driver. And they did, along with our luggage. When we were a safe distance away, my daughter and I held each other tightly. "Way to go, Mom," said Ali.

As you can see, at times like this, the Soldier is imminently useful. He has many looks and forms and shapes. Marty and Pat particularly like the cartoon character *Shrek* who is another portrayal of the Soldier. He is gruff on the outside but will do anything to rescue those he loves and keep them from harm. Just look at what he was willing to do for Fiona! Pat also likes the images of the Soldier portrayed in the leading roles in the movies *Braveheart*, *The Patriot*, and *Gladiator*. Marty's favorite Warrior I is the Terminator, from the movie *Terminator I*. His motto is, "If you are trouble, you are finished."

Your own inner Soldier can take many forms and shapes. At times, Pat likes to imagine hers as a Native American male. Once he came forward as a big, bald guy named Huey.

Exercise: Close your eyes and see or hear or feel the forms and shapes in which you experience your inner Soldier. Write down a description of him or her in the following space.

Good! Now you know your Soldier better. And you might even want to thank him for how he helps you in the world, and for the ways he has protected you and those you love.

But no matter how useful the Soldier has been or can be, know that he is certain to show up when we experience the Oh Shit! shame, and he must never be turned loose on the ones we love. He has no place in Loveland. Remember, Loveland is defined as a place in which there is an absence of malice. The alpha man or woman will always hear their Soldier whispering things like "Kill 'em!" or "Shoot first, ask questions later," or "Shut them up." In Loveland, this is a malicious presence. As much as we don't want it to, this presence will turn on our partner during difficult, challenging, and uncomfortable times. He does not belong in Loveland. "When In Doubt, Rub It Out" is the wrong song to sing in Loveland. He belongs outside the door to our home, protecting us and the ones we love.

Your coach can and must learn to control your Soldier, or you are going to continue to be a loose cannon during another short sojourn in Loveland. In a relationship with a good person, Soldier is there to protect the outer perimeters of our relationship and to protect both of us from the bad guys who want to mess with us or with those we love. And as coach, you must never give up your leadership position to your Soldier. He's got to work for you. If he is in charge of the team, he will become a tyrant.

You can draw on your experience of team sports, in which the competitive warrior does his best to win but also respects the rules that determine where and how hard you can hit. In team sports, even with blood in your eye, you play by the rules or you will get thrown out of the park on a technical.

For alpha women reading this book, we hope that you have also had the advantage of having played team sports. In any event, alpha women often learn to manage this warrior part by grouping with other alpha women, where their warrior is supported and there are group guidelines for how and when to exercise their Soldier. Unfortunately, all too often, the most allowable target is the most available male. And that's not okay; it does not promote intimacy.

For guys who are involved with alpha women, you must understand the following: Alpha women all run in packs. If you love one, you're going to deal with more than one, often eventually all the women in her pack. If you offend the women in her pack, you're going to offend her. If you offend her, you're going to have to deal with the women in her pack. Ever listened to that Dixie Chicks song "Earl's Gotta Die?", about Earl? You should. If your Warrior I (Warrior I is the Soldier, Warrior II is the Secret Agent) ever offends your alpha female partner, her rat pack is gonna be singing "Earl's Gotta Die." About you.

Warrior II: The Secret Agent

Not every alpha gets genetically issued a Secret Agent. If you have one, you know it, because you can outfox the best of them. This is the team player who knows that if he can't blind 'em with brilliance, then he can always baffle 'em with impenetrable stratagems (aka very dressed-up bullshit). What's his plan? As outlined in *The Forty-Eight Laws of Power* by Robert Greene, his plan is to maintain power through any means necessary, and to not get caught at it, while appearing to be loving and gentle. His motto is, "Love is not the solution; love is the problem."

[Caveat: If you do not have this kind of warrior within, you will be repulsed by our descriptions and stories. Conversely, if you cannot stop yourself from reading this and are highly repulsed, you probably have one that you haven't admitted to yet. Marty's wife, Leslie, said that she found these last two warrior types so repugnant that she would never have finished reading the book if she hadn't loved the authors so much. If you have a Warrior I/Soldier but not a Warrior II/Secret Agent or a Warrior III/Bitch/Bastard from Hell, skip the next two sections.]

When present, this team member is genetic in alphas, whether it is elicited or not. It is not elicited by bad upbringing. He can often be elicited by hard times, especially hard times in which we are betrayed by those we have trusted, those we believed loved us. This guy uses the horror stories of our childhood and early love life in which we were misused and humiliated to justify protecting us from ever being hurt like that again. He knows that the biggest risk of pain in life, and the one you should avoid at all costs, comes from the people you love and trust. He or she knows that love entraps people, weakens their will to survive, and allows them to be treated as fools. In defense against vulnerability, he is never really going to let you give your heart away. He will, if you allow him, have you hold back, keep secrets, quietly betray, keep one foot in and one foot out of a relationship through a secret back door, and in any way necessary keep you out of Loveland. Unfortunately, when you meet the right person to love, he will especially block that.

> George and Mary Ann had been married for eighteen years. The first years of their marriage had been blissful ones. Inevitably, in the fourth year of their marriage, the challenges of negotiating differences and life stresses began to present themselves. George felt inept in addressing these. He began to avoid Mary Ann's persistent attempts to talk about their problems. Their interactions at home became more and more "polite" and on the surface, looked like a scene from *The Brady Bunch*. However, the juice was gone from their relationship. Each focused on raising their two children and on their careers. The year after their second child left for college, the emptiness in their relationship became more pronounced. George spent longer-than-usual hours at work and often told Mary Ann that he was pursuing his musical hobbies

on evenings and weekends. One day, a friend approached Mary Ann and awkwardly told her of seeing George in a bar, intimately conversing with another woman. Upon questioning George, Mary Ann was shocked to find that George had been having affairs for ten years.

The Secret Agent uses his Machiavellian strategies in pursuing the challenge of destroying love without getting caught at it. And since the ultimate goal of the challenge is to escape the vulnerability of love and to survive, the end justifies any means. The Secret Agent is death to love. He glories in the death of love. He is good at forming alliances, and yet is good at scheming and holding back, in the service of his own survival. When love gets in the way of that, he pulls out, or he betrays his partner so that the partner pulls out.

To show you how subtle the Secret Agent is, we're going to look at alpha women with Secret Agents on their inner team. Why them? Because their Secret Agent is even more subtle than in guys. How do they do it? Here are some formulas, actual stories from Marty's psychiatry practice:

1. "Fall in love" with people you know you are not going to marry, and do not tell them that you are not going to marry them. Wait until the guy is on bended knee, having fully convinced himself that you are the love of his life. Then tell him.

2. Pick guys who are clearly inappropriate and/or unavailable and then work years with your therapist to turn a frog into a prince. The certain failure burns up the years while you are avoiding the very difficult work of being truly vulnerable. Finally, you can convince yourself that you are "too old to be marketable."

3. Marry a guy who's unlovable but makes a good living and good social appearance. Be the "devoted wife"; take no risks.

Here is how the Secret Agent worked in one woman.

Gladys adored her father. When she was four years old, her father left the family one night without a word. Heartbroken, she vowed she would never be hurt like this again. She became a successful marketing executive where she met and formed relationships with a string of men. She began each relationship with a pretense of loving, and she pretended well. Often she even fooled herself. Secretly she never let her partners get too close. To her, each relationship was a business deal. Her secret goals for each of these deals depended on what she wanted at that particular time in her life. It might be a man who could help her get a promotion, or one who could help her ward off loneliness on the weekends, or one who would be a good travel companion on vacations. When her goals were no longer met or when she moved on to other goals, she discarded her current partner and searched for a new one.

The Secret Agent is not intrinsically mean. He is devoted to your survival, and if allowed, will use any means possible. Outside an intimate relationship, in his most positive form, the Secret Agent wants to be free, ennobled, empowered, and admired.

Another good example of a Warrior II/Secret Agent is the character of the woman hospital administrator in the movie *John Q*. Her end goal is to make the most profit for the hospital. She doesn't seem mean. She even puts on an amicable face when it serves her efforts to achieve her goals. But any love is scorned, dismissed by her. She turns a deaf ear when John Q speaks from his heart about saving his son. Only when John Q mobilizes his inner Warrior I and the publicity and consequent profit for the hospital is threatened does the Secret Agent/Hospital Administrator allow John's son to receive the heart transplant necessary for saving his life.

If you work in a competitive, cutthroat workplace or other political environment in which making deals and alliances for the achievement of your own goals is necessary, the Secret Agent is a necessary member of your team. Don't work in a situation like that unless you have one, because the motto is "At the poker table, if you don't know who "the sucker is, Guess Who? It's You." For the full text, read Robert Greene's *The Forty-Eight Laws of Power*. Following his instructions, you can trick anyone out of anything while "happily" living a seemingly "loving" life.

If you have a Secret Agent/Warrior II on your committee, it must be parked outside the gates of Loveland, just like Warrior I/Soldier. He can be useful in protecting your relationship and life against crooked salespeople or others who might try to take advantage of you and he can be useful in the business world, but he should never be let loose against the one you love.

Exercise: Recall a past triumph, gained through subterfuge. They thought they had you, but you slipped away. You were Hannibal Lector in Silence of the Lambs. You were the Kevin Spacey character in the movie The Usual Suspects. You were Leonardo di Capprio in Catch Me if You Can. You were the Road Runner. Beep Beep!

Remember emotions of quiet excitement and glee in your triumph. Fully remember the feelings of being "one-up," and able to walk away. Write about this.

Now, check to see if you ever lied, were sneaky, withheld facts, withheld your heart, and felt consequently superior in a loving relationship, especially if you got away with it. Write about this.

If you found that you did the above things in a loving relationship, your toughest struggle will be with the Secret Agent, because now you know that he is the problem. Conversely, he now knows that you are the problem, because now you are onto him. We hope you win. You need to if you want to stay in Loveland because if you, the coach of the Love Team, are not in charge, the Secret Agent is, and the Power Team is winning.

Warrior III: The Sadistic Bastard and Bitch From Hell

Thankfully, Warrior III is found less frequently than the other two. Marty sometimes calls this "The Mean Gene." This is the most dangerous of the three warriors. In the movie, Terminator III, this character was played by a woman-faced robot, literally the Bitch from Hell. In the movie *Fatal Attraction*, Glenn Close frightened an entire generation of married men with boiled bunny. The classic blonde-haired, blue-eyed Nazi officer in an endless number of American World War II movies who enjoys tormenting his victims and then is contemptuous of them once they are dead is an example of this warrior.

Warrior III likes to destroy people and actually enjoys seeing the suffering of others. This is the core of sadism. This warrior is the predator cat that plays with its food. If you have ever tangled with one of these, you found out that you were food. If you have a Warrior III within, the worse you were treated as a child (perhaps by a parent who was also cursed by this team member on their inner committee) the stronger your cruelty will be. Some very primitive part of you believes "misery loves company." You want people to experience how badly you have been hurt. You hurt others for the sake of hurting, enjoying the process and feeling somehow comforted when you witness the hurt you inflict on others.

Warrior III may also take more subtle forms, like the person who enjoys springing unpleasant surprises on others and then enjoys watching their confusion and agony. This is the wife who arranges for her husband to find her in the arms of another man and enjoys his shock and humiliation.

If you have a Warrior III and want to live in Loveland, your inner coach will not be enough. You will need to have a professional coach (a very good therapist), who will teach you how to be in charge, someone who has the necessary and unusual expertise to help clients master this monstrous team member. Because at least one of your parents was probably abusive to you, you must look for a therapist who can help you explore and develop compassion for the child who was wounded. Otherwise it will be impossible for you to contain your own nastiness. You must heal your hurt before you will be able to stop hurting others. You need a therapist who can help you recognize and exclude any behavior of this inner committee member in personal or business relationships. Only muggers and other criminals deserve this nasty side of you. In the meantime, as coach, you and any other committee members (Soldier can be helpful here), may need to lock this committee member in a dark closet. If you are in Loveland with a good partner and have Warrior III, what is it good for? Only one thing: terrorizing a terrorist that invades your home.

Warrior Styles

While one or all of the warriors described above are genetically endowed primordial clay of the alpha, the genetic drives that originate from these warriors can act in the world through one or more strategies or positions. Ludeman and Erlandson in their book *Alpha Male Syndrome* have described and characterized various styles that alphas in leadership positions can take (pp. 48-51). They are:

The Commander:

Strengths
-Has an abundance of energy
-Good at motivating people and getting them to perform well
-Persuasive speaker
-Charismatic

Risks
-Hardly ever shows vulnerability
-Can be highly argumentative
-Can be harsh and overly direct when stressed or worried about something
-Occasionally bends the rules or spins the truth to accomplish what they want
-Pushes self hard to surpass the performance of others
-Often feels jealous of peers who outperform them or gain more recognition, although they may not show it

The Visionary:

Strengths
-Excels at starting new projects and allowing others to finish
-Often comes up with breakthrough ideas
-When making important decisions, has learned he is right to trust his gut
-Likes finding new ways to do things rather than taking the accepted route
-Is more innovative than practical
-Enjoys working in situations that demand improvisation

Risks
-Gets caught up in what's new and loses interest in routine work
-Sometimes has unrealistic expectations when starting new projects
-Starts new projects before finishing old ones
-Gets frustrated dealing with naysayers and worrywarts
-Finds that achieving his vision usually takes more time and resources than he anticipated

The Strategist:

Strengths

-Is very analytic, logical, and data-oriented in decision-making
-Operates from mental maps that allow him to pull important data together
-Doesn't allow emotions to affect his decisions
-Has laser-like focus once he locks onto something
-Is praised for his intellectual horsepower
-Can come up with the right decision if he has the data

Risks

-Doesn't like selling his ideas; thinks people should be able to recognize the superiority of his ideas
-Has little respect for people who space out or get confused easily
-Believes he doesn't need input from others to make good decisions
-Can almost always find a logical flaw with someone else's argument
-Doesn't go out of his way to develop relationships at work; focuses on getting the job done
-Focuses more on getting good results and less on how people feel
-Tends to make mental leaps and gets annoyed when people can't follow him

The Executor:

Strengths

-When he begins a project, immediately sees the steps that must be taken to succeed
-Provides clear goals and expectations to those who work below him
-Before starting a project, makes sure that a clear timeline and detailed plan of action are in place
-Likes it when work projects follow a strict and reliable schedule
-When he delegates, follows up to make sure everything is on track
-Likes team members to give him frequent updates

Risks

-Even when in a leadership role, tends to get involved in the details
-Has been accused of being a "control freak"
-Doesn't spend much time celebrating success
-Rarely finds the work of others up to his standards
-Can be very critical when he sees problems in someone's work
-Gets irritated when people miss deadlines, don't keep agreements, or skip significant details

For those who are alphas in business or who are dealing with alphas in business, we recommend *Alpha Male Syndrome*. Ludeman and Erlandman's book complements our book by describing how to be an alpha in a positive way in business and how to deal with alphas in business; ours focuses on personal relationships.

In our description of the warriors and Ludeman and Erlandson's description of how these warriors are expressed in different alpha styles, we see that alphas can look very different from one another while continuing to express their alpha nature. Just as in the movies, alphas can look very different from one another because of costume, era, location, and complementary characters. But make no mistake; they are still being in the world from their warrior places.

Further, alphas not yet committed to life in Loveland tend to be shifty. They lie about being fully committed, while always keeping some part of their heart uncommitted and some options secretly open for other opportunities. Different alpha types have different values they consider most rewarding. Whatever that highest value is, alphas are addicted to it. Some seek power, some seek fame, some seek sloth (even sloth is a prize, mostly for those with inherited wealth), some money, some sex, some getting high on adrenaline or other mind-altering substances. Some seek righteousness, and some seek omniscience (they are the know-it-alls). So, when you see an actual alpha in front of you, whether in the mirror or elsewhere, he will be decked out in a particular way and ready for a particular kind of action. These different forms can be given cute nicknames that capture our action-hero at play but clearly are neither genetic nor driven by culture, except as culture provides the choices. Consequently, these characters are more easily controlled than the genetically driven warriors or even the long-practiced strategies that become habitual.

For example, Earl, a prisoner Marty knew as warden and psychiatrist at the U.S. Penitentiary in Marion, Illinois, was in prison for bank robbery. After attending Marty's classes, Earl set about to use his warriors, including his Secret Agent, to look good to the review board so he could con them into parole. He became one of Marty's few failures. Charles Kuralt was another good example. He appeared to be a model of the stand-up guy roving reporter. After his death, the world was shocked when his will revealed that he had been married to two women, each in a different part of the country. His first wife knew nothing of the second wife. For alphas, the costumes change, the behaviors change, but the genetic traits and acquired strategies remain the same.

In summary, there are four layers of understanding about alphas. There are the **genetic drivers**. There are the **styles** with which the drivers express themselves as illustrated in Ludeman's and Erlandson's work including Commander, Executor, Visionary and Strategist. There are the **prizes** mentioned above, including money, inappropriate sexual exploits, sloth, status, and attributed omniscience. Finally, there are the variations of how these get played out in costume, behavior, and style, depending on the context in which the alpha finds himself.

Layers of the Warrior
(Cultural Manifestations Vary With Context)

Genetic Types	Styles	Sorting Mechanisms/Prizes
I. Warrior I: Soldier (Every alpha has At least this one)	Commander	Money
	Visionary	Status
II. Secret Agent	Strategist	Sexual Exploits
III. Sadistic Bastard/Bitch From Hell	Executor	Reputation for High Skill Levels
		Reputation for Best Provider
		Reputation for Integrity
		Reputation for Effective Protector
		Sloth (When Rich)

About Female Alphas

Female alphas, by definition, have their Inner Warrior(s) too. Our culture encourages and rewards male alphas. They are considered "normal." Not so for women; in fact, until recently, it was dangerous for young girls and adult women to demonstrate alpha traits. At best, you were considered "not a real girl." At worst, demonstrating your alpha qualities was an invitation to be "put in your place" through verbal put-downs, physical abuse, rape, and in some instances, death. For this reason, many females, especially those older than 45, when they learn that they are alpha, deny their alpha nature and stubbornly resist any suggestion that they are. They do this despite their large and obvious interest in, and desire for, leadership and action in their lives. While they may be competitive in sports, they often deny this, and at work may be covertly competitive. Culturally trained to value relationships, they hide until they are riled, and then lie about being competitive. Then they fight for survival with the best.

Ludeman and Erlandson refer to a Fortune magazine article, "The Art of the Decision," which states that women are more likely than their male counterparts to collaborate, listen, and try to build teams in the workplace. The workplace is a public place with a public face; behind closed doors in their personal partnerships, alpha females can come out as fiercely as any alpha guy. They may try to bludgeon their beta partner, or even a weaker alpha partner, into submission, to prove that they are not competitive. Or they will pull tricks and use rhetoric. Do not let them fool you. Their gentleness, when evident, is decisional, like any male alpha's. They can change on a dime and fight. If you are a male involved with an alpha female, all meanness that you experience will be described as "your fault" and invite more meanness if confronted.

Other Non-Warrior Committee Members

As we have said, most alphas will have at least one and maybe two or three of the Warrior committee members. There are many other committee members, some of which are unique to each individual. Getting to know these can be interesting and often useful as we navigate our relationships and our broader world. A good book about this is *Embracing Ourselves: The Voice Dialogue Manual* by Hal and Sidra Stone(2001).

There are several other almost universal committee members who should be mentioned here, because, in addition to the Warrior(s), they will be influencing us as we join our partner in addressing relationship difficulties. Some of these are adopted from Transactional Analysis literature.

The Free Child

This is the joyful, fun, playful part of our self. If we are lucky, this part has been there since we were little. It plays an important role in our inner committee. Hal and Siddra in their book, *Embracing Ourselves:The Voice Dialogue Manual,* (2001) say that it is impossible to be in a good intimate relationship without our free children being engaged with each other.

This part of us often gets activated when we first fall in love. We hold hands, we skip, we laugh, and we *play* together.

Our free child can often help to dispel a tense situation. Even the Soldier is susceptible to the free child's honesty. Our free child can be brought into a tense encounter with our partner to help disarm our Warrior, or our partner's Warrior. However, the honest and caring humor of the free child should not be confused with the sarcastic humor of Powerland members of our committee.

Another reason it is helpful to pay attention to our Free Child in our inner committee is because the free child loves to go out and play at inappropriate times. When we encounter a problem in our relationship, it is not time for the free child to jump into the coach's chair with, "Oh, let's forget this and go to the beach (get a hot dog, go golfing, make love, go to the fair, etc.)" Those are the times that our coach hears that the Free Child would prefer to go play than be in this particular situation right now. The coach can promise the Free Child that we will play later (And keep the promise!) and then get on about the awkward business of problem solving with our partner.

The Adaptive Child/Scared Little Boy or Girl

The Adaptive Child is the part of us that learned to be good, to cave in, and to not speak up in order to avoid harm. This harm may have come in the form of being shamed, or made fun of, or belittled. It may have even come in the form of physical harm, such as beatings.

Even though alphas have one or more Warriors on their committee, they may very well have an Adaptive Child. This is especially true if we have grown up in a family where there was intimidation and bullying or too much strictness. In fact, sometimes our Warrior is developed in order to protect the Adaptive Child, or the Warrior may have copied our bullying parent and now the bullying parent is on our inner committee in the form of the Warrior, along with the Adaptive Child.

If our partner exhibits Powerland behavior, our Adaptive Child may want to jump into the coach's chair. It may whisper things to us such as, "Just do whatever they say," "Don't rock the boat," or, "Just drop it; don't speak up." In relationships when we allow our Adaptive Child to take over, we lose our self-esteem; we diminish ourselves and our ability to address the problems head on. We also allow our partner's Powerland behavior to rule. We eventually become resentful of this. And the problems don't get solved.

Our Adaptive Child may also get activated when our own inner Powerland players get out of line for too long and our partner sets limits, withdraws, or begins to question whether they have the heart to stay in a relationship with us.

> John had thrown one too many temper tantrums. His wife Maria began to wonder if she could stay in the relationship. She shared these feelings with John. Instead of working on controlling his temper tantrums, John brought his wife an expensive necklace, accompanied with the words, "I'm sorry. I'll be good."

This kind of behavior can be very confusing to a partner who is looking for an apology. What you must look at here is whether your partner's contriteness is genuine, and if they really want to take responsibility for bad behavior by doing something to change it, or whether they are just placating and hoping to avoid abandonment from the Adaptive Child position.

The Nurturing Parent

The Nurturing Parent is an inner committee member who really knows how to take care of a child. This inner member knows how to put us to bed early when we have had a rough day, feed us good food, take the Free Child out to play and soothe us when we are troubled.

In healthy relationships, we sometimes use our Nurturing Parent to soothe our partner after a hard day at the office or in times of great vulnerability. This is fine, if it happens bilaterally and if it is not the major interaction in the relationship. It can be a problem if we expect our mate to assume that role for us instead of developing our own self-care capacities. Difficult problems result if we feel that we are *entitled* to our partner's becoming a constant Nurturing Parent.

The Compassionate/Empathetic One

This is an inner committee member who may be more easily accessible if you are an alpha female or a beta male who has been trained to act like an alpha male. It is more present in women because even alpha women are socialized to be understanding and caring. It is more inherent in all betas, either men or women.

The Compassionate/Empathetic One understands the heart of pain. She/he is the one who knows in their gut that underneath most bad behavior is pain and shame. The Compassionate One can be a very useful member on one's inner committee in the service of partnership. If we have behaved badly, the Compassionate One helps us to understand the pain and shame from which our bad behavior came. This helps us to understand and forgive ourself, which makes it easier to ask forgiveness and explain ourself to our partner. It helps us to not stay stuck in self-righteously defending our bad behavior. It also helps us to forgive our partner, because as the Compassionate One understands our own pain and shame, it also understands the pain and shame in our partner.

While the Compassionate/Empathetic One can be an indispensable ally, it can also be dangerous in relationships, particularly if we put our partner first in a situation in which we should be taking care of ourselves. It can also be dangerous if it jumps into the coach's chair and encourages us to tolerate abusive behavior because it understands the abuser's pain.

The Adult

The Adult, in Transactional Analysis literature, is more narrowly defined than we customarily use it in general culture, when we say, "Be an adult." Neurophysiologically, the Adult originates in the left prefrontal cortex; it includes the best information we have available about the reality of things. It is the part of us that reads training manuals and IRS instructions. The Adult has a rationally chosen ethical base that may be overridden by either emotional and/or belief-driven ethics from other areas of the brain during stress. Because the Adult works slowly and methodically, it often is not operative under stressful conditions.

Empathy comes from the right brain and consists of standing in the other person's shoes; it is a role-model form of learning about the source of the other person's distress. To the distressed person, empathy feels like they are being understood. We can report the same kind of understanding, in a cognitive way, from the Adult, but to the distressed person who is requesting empathy, it feels cold and indifferent. The Adult doesn't have feelings; it learns, receives, stores, processes and conveys information.

The Adult member of our inner committee can be useful to our partner by conveying information that might clear up a misunderstanding.

> Brenda felt abandoned when her husband Brad was an hour late for a dinner date. When he appeared, she lapsed into a tirade about how he didn't care about her feelings. Brad responded from the Compassionate/Empathetic committee member, conveying that he understood how she felt. Then, from his Adult, he gave her the information that there had been a traffic-immobilizing wreck on the freeway, and that he had no choice but to wait until traffic moved again.

The Adult is not useful if it begins spouting facts when the partner needs listening or needs a response from the Compassionate/Empathetic committee member. It can even be destructive.

The Nerd Scientist/Anthropologist

The Nerd Scientist/Anthropologist is an upgraded expansion of the Adult. This committee member may get advanced training from reading, attending workshops, scientific training, and intellectually analyzed life experiences. At its highest level, he has had scientific training, and he acts as if he is not human; he acts as an intelligent alien, studying the human race, driven by unconnectful curiosity and modeling the "natives" somewhat mechanically and stiffly. Just like Mr. Spock in Star Trek, he does have his human side. It just embarrasses and baffles him and he would rather the human side didn't come out. If he is allowed to take over the coach's role, he moves to an arm's length from, and not part of, the human race. If you are a high level cognitive professional, one way that you can misuse this book is as a guide to manipulating and managing others. If the thought has already occurred to you, take heed.

This is a committee member who forages into Loveland as an anthropologist would go into a foreign country out of scientific interest in learning the ways of its citizens. He disguises himself as a citizen of that country and lives among the inhabitants of that country until the going gets rough. Read more about him in the Epilogue: My Trip to Deadwood.

Non-Warrior Committee Members

Name	Partnership Assets	Partnership Liabilities
Free Child	Helps dispel tense situations Builds closeness through play Disarms warriors	Can play at inappropriate times, eg. when attending to a relationship problem should be a priority Can distract from problem-solving
Adaptive/ Scared Child		Avoids addressing problems Causes low self-esteem and feelings of unworthiness to state needs Allows Powerland behavior to Rule Placates instead of problem-solving or giving genuine apology
Nurturing Parent	Helps soothe self and partner	If used unilaterally, encourages one partner to overdepend instead of developing their own Nurturing Parent

Compassionate/ Empathetic One	Helps us understand and forgive ourselves when we behave badly Does same for partner Helps us explain ourself to and ask forgiveness from our partner Helps us get unstuck from self-righteous defensiveness Helps us understand and forgive our partner	Can be dangerous if always putting partner first when should be attending to self Can be dangerous if fosters tolerance of abuse secondary to feeling compassion for pain of abuser
Adult	Conveys information that may help clear up a misunderstanding	Can coldly spout facts in situations better served by empathy If attempts to convey empathy, feels cold and indifferent to partner
Nerd Scientist/ Anthropologist		Forages in Loveland disguised as citizen to satisfy scientific curiosity Unconnectful curiosity for sake of learning and possible manipulation Keeps us at arm's length of partner

Highest Level of Skill

Part of the commitment to absence of malice involves a commitment to not knowingly, willfully, or negligently do bad, stupid, or hurtful things. Beyond not doing these kinds of things, you need to make a commitment to use your highest level of skill. Each of us must make a commitment to use our highest level of skill. What does this mean?

By the time we reach a period in our lives during which we think about havng a second chance at a good relationship, we have spent some time in extremely adverse circumstances. These circumstances include dealing with difficult people in relationships at work, in church groups, or in volunteer settings. Many of these activities have challenged us and provided lessons and useful skills we need in order to make an intimate relationship and live in Loveland. Beyond not killing someone in all the subtle or not so subtle ways possible, other useful skills we have learned include communicating, negotiating, exploring, patience, and empathy.

For example, we may have had times when we thought our boss was being really stupid, when we may have had momentary fantasies of "punching out his or her lights," or turning and walking out the door with a loud, "I quit!".

We managed ourselves; we especially managed one or more of our warriors who could have destroyed our job with one giant, "Take this job and shove it." We took a deep breath and asked the boss to explain more about his idea, even if it seemed stupid to us. We tactfully questioned decisions. We politely told him or her that we have a suggestion. We swallowed pride and apologized for mistakes. We stayed in the room when we really wanted to storm out, slamming the door behind us. All of these skills are part of bringing our highest and best to a situation. At times, we even found that the boss or a fellow employee or volunteer knew something that we didn't know, something that was useful and important. If we hadn't kept our mouth shut and asked questions and practiced empathy, we would have never found out. And we may have lost our job.

As alphas, we typically act better in work, team sports, or even community program situations, than we do in our marriages. If you truly want a second chance, you really must bring this your highest and best to your intimate relationships. Remember, in Loveland, everyone is innocent until proven guilty. *Everyone has a contribution to make.*

"I do too much of that at work; that's what they pay me for," you may say. "My home, my love life, that's a place where I want to relax, and be myself!"

Our answer is to ask you the following question: Why would you want to use a lower level of skill in your marriage, or intimate partnership, when you are capable of using a higher level of skill in other contexts? Any answer other than a willingness to do your best is unacceptable. If you say you love your partner, that you are committed, and that you want your relationship to work, why would you purposefully go about using anything less than your highest level of skill? What kind of logic is that? To act dumb and dangerous in relationship is a form of what Alcoholics' Anonymous calls "Stinkin' Thinkin' ."

In review, these are the commitments that you must make in order to operate with an absence of malice and to use your highest level of skill with your partner. They include the commitment to:

> Remind ourselves that no one is coercing us to be here, that we volunteered for the job, that it is something we want that requires an increase in our skill level as we head forward in facing this problem with our partner.
>
> Develop and use a strong coach for our inner team, especially the Warriors.
>
> Park our Powerland Warriors outside the door to our home and use them for protection, for the well being of our loved ones, never for harm.
>
> Have our coach appropriately keep any other committee members who are not useful from coming front and center.
>
> Avoid negative conclusions about our partner's motivations; see ourselves, our partner, and the relationship in the best possible light. Each is innocent until proven guilty, unless malice has entered the relationship.
>
> Use our highest level of skill in our intimate partnership.

There is one more commitment that must be put in place before beginning the process of living in Loveland. That is a commitment to continuous connection. As you will discover, this requires your highest level of skill and deserves a chapter all its own. Please read on.

CHAPTER SEVEN

THE COMMITMENT TO CONTINUOUS CONNECTION

Loveland is a place of continuous connection. Continuous connection is not the same as continuous contact. We can feel deeply connected to our partner when we are at work, in a different country, or in any other way separate from them. Some people experience this connection in a strong psychic way, such as knowing what the other is about to say, or knowing when they are particularly distressed or happy, even if they are miles away.

When we experience the Oh Shit! moment and *Whoosh!* to Powerland, a disconnect occurs. The next commitment that must be made in a loving partnership is to immediately attend to the disconnect. A disconnect is always a crisis in a relationship. Some disconnects can become a relationship train wreck, if not attended to. Some disconnects are already train wrecks by the time you notice them. We define train wreck as any big mess that happens in a relationship. It is more damaging than a disconnect. You are going happily along on your way, either alone or with your partner, in either case enjoying your connection to yourself and/or your connection to your partner. Out of the blue comes the Oh Shit! moment which, if allowed to escalate, could become a train wreck.

If you are smart and lucky, commitment to attend to these moments of crisis may be agreed upon early in the relationship, while you are still in the honeymoon stage. Alternatively it may be made as part of damage control after cleaning up the debris from an early relationship train wreck. But eventually, in order for you to live in Loveland, *you must commit to continuous connection.* Loveland is, by definition, continuous connection.

A disconnect that is not self-healing is a crisis. Not self-healing means that for one or both of the partners, one or more warriors take charge and treat the event as a survival issue in which they need to dominate in order to survive. They treat the situation as a fight/flight/freeze problem as opposed to a tend and befriend problem.

There are some crises that can never be anticipated, especially early in the relationship. As the honeymoon phase of the relationship wanes, couples begin to discover their differences.

> Susan and John met when they were in their early 60's. Each had lived alone for some period of time. Susan was a widow who, after mourning her late husband's death, had enjoyed living alone. She had a wide circle of friends and relatives who were a critical part of her happiness. She and her late husband had each been active in their professional lives and valued times when they engaged in activities outside their marriage as much as they valued their times together. When John unexpectedly came into her life, she was smitten, much to her surprise. They had many common interests and values and explored the viability of a relationship.
>
> John had been divorced for ten years. John was very extroverted, a connector, a people person. He did not like living alone and yearned for partnership in his life. His parents, whose marriage he admired, had worked together and shared most of their waking moments in only each other's company. John held to the strong belief that intimacy should be limited to the marriage relationship. Susan did not share that belief, and had multiple close friendships.
>
> One day soon after John and Susan began living together, Susan announced that she was going to her quilting club that evening. Unexpectedly, John whooshed to Powerland. He began berating Susan for activity outside their partnership, accusing her of living a "single life" and lecturing her about how a partnership "should be," based on his observations of his parents' marriage. Susan took her own jet plane to Powerland, proclaiming that no man was going to tell her what to do. She then initiated her own lecture about what a relationship should look like. In a crisis of disappointed expectations, they were experiencing a train wreck.

Sometimes train wrecks *can* be anticipated, particularly as a couple gains experience with each other and as a partnership team. Here is a story about how Marty and Leslie gained understanding and experience after a train wreck. As it turned out, their ability to address the first disconnect around this issue saved Marty's life.

> Marty fights cancer. He fights cancer in the same way he approaches other aspects of his life: he researches related literature broadly and deeply, even to the point of joining the American Society for Clinical Oncology; he constructs the most effective strategy for himself that he can; he applies his innate and sharpened brilliance of mind; he engages his strong personality and determination.
>
> For his physicians, he is not the usual cancer patient. In addition to his being acutely aware of anti-cancer medications and side effects, his strong personality can be very convincing, even on the basis of false hope. He is frequently, and not to his advantage, able to shut up his physicians by doggedly sticking to his point of view. His point of view regarding treatment is not always the most useful one.
>
> In most situations, Marty's doctors did not have the time, energy, or skill to override him. Instead, after a few trials of presenting opinions different than Marty's, they shut up. By mutual agreement, Marty's wife, Leslie, a nurse, accompanied Marty to his clinic visits. She would sometimes be silently agreeing with the doctors and found herself emotionally disconnecting from Marty when he would doggedly disagree with and override his physicians.
>
> After a particularly critical visit, when Marty had repeated his override behavior and Leslie experienced a crisis of disconnection, Leslie initiated a discussion in response to her disconnect. *Remember, if one person experiences a disconnect, there is a disconnect. By definition, continuous connection must be experienced by both partners.* In response to Leslie's initiation of this crisis discussion, Marty realized that there was a pattern in his behavior that was not useful. They devised a plan to address this pattern. (We will tell you more about making plans in later chapters.)
>
> Here is the plan that Marty and Leslie constructed: With Marty's permission, when Leslie noticed that Marty was not listening to his physicians and was overriding them in ways that seemed deleterious to his treatment, she would call a time out. Her words to the physician were the following: "My husband and I need to consult on this before we proceed. Would you please listen?" Leslie would then discuss with Marty her understanding of the doctor's point of view, consulting with the physician for information or confirmation of her understanding.

May 31, 2003, was a turning point in Marty's and Leslie's life, because their plan, which had evolved after the first disconnect discussion, saved Marty's life. He had been resisting major surgery (a permanent colostomy) for months. Now it was an emergency. Leslie initiated their time-out plan and got Marty to listen and understand the danger of any further delay. As a result, Marty was admitted the next morning for the life-saving surgery. After the successful surgery, the surgeon said to Marty, "If I had been as sick as you were the day before the emergency surgery, I would be dead."

Years later, Marty and Leslie have enjoyed many sweet moments in their life journey together, moments they would have missed if they had ignored the original disconnect. It is easy to lose courage, or to be lazy or passive, or to think that perhaps a disconnect is not important and can be ignored, but ignoring a loose wheel on a train is a choice that can be disastrous.

Stop The Train, The Wheel Is Loose!

A disconnect occurs and the mutually agreed-upon signal is given to announce the crisis. A requirement of our commitment to continuous connection is that at this point, any further expectations of normality (business as usual) stop. The crisis is now the focus of the relationship, except for emergencies and childcare.

Ordinary life is going on and suddenly there is a disconnect--by definition, a crisis. At this point, you negotiate about time and space to resolve the crisis. If you are fortunate, you have time in the present. Life, however, is not always so convenient and can interfere. There is usually already an agenda, a plan. You may be on your way to the dentist or people may be coming for dinner. If it is an event involving you both as a couple, negotiate when, after the event, you will begin to discuss the crisis. If it is an individual obligation, negotiate when that will be completed and both parties will be available for the necessary discussion. You are not necessarily obligated to fix the problem at the moment of crisis, because that may not be practically or emotionally feasible.

The obligation is to make a commitment to fix it either now or when practical, preferably some time in the next 24 hours when both of you will be available, able to focus on the crisis and have enough time to deal with it, whatever that may take.

Given the fact that neither of you know how long resolving the problem is going to take, open your heart to infinite patience. What is infinite patience? Having infinite patience means mustering, in advance of the discussion, more patience than is needed, when you don't know how much that is going to be. (See Chapter Fifteen, on Self-Soothing.) So, if you are on your way to the dentist, it is not a good time. When you start unpacking one of these crises, it could take ten minutes, or it could take the afternoon. If you are sitting on the porch having a conversation and someone says some snotty, shitty thing, you can stop right there and process it. If people are due for dinner in thirty minutes, you will need to agree to set a time as soon as you can.

Whenever possible, it is especially important to resolve issues within the following 24 hours. This is however difficult because generally an alpha's initial response to crisis is anger, if not rage, whether behaviorally expressed or not. The neurophysiological experience of anger/rage includes an increase in stress hormones, adrenalin, and cortisol, and a decrease in serotonin. Serotonin helps us maintain our equilibrium. In the absence of any further negative stimuli (such as provocation by your partner) these anger-induced neurophysiological changes take 24 hours to clear. Worse yet, our most paranoid illusions about the motivation of our partners are released by these neurophysiological changes. We are programmed to assess potential dangers on a worst-case scenario basis, as if our survival is endangered. Our warriors, whichever are present, eagerly step forward to self-righteously fight the good fight against our newfound enemy, our love. If we allow our warriors to intervene on our behalf, our simple domestic crisis becomes a train wreck. *Our recommendation is to do the hardest thing you can do, which is to have your coach stay in charge, calm and soothe yourself, use your highest levels of skill, and do not let your warriors intervene.*

Resolving disconnects quickly is also good for your physical health. Janice Kiecolt-Glaser, PhD, lead author of a study of 42 married couples (Archives of General Psychiatry, 2005, 1377) found that even low-level stress from a minor disagreement with a spouse can delay wound healing after surgery by a day, a major disagreement by two days. Hostility hinders the regulation of cytokine, an important chemical in the immune system. When cytokine stays in the blood too long, it results in increased inflammation, which slows healing. Further, people who feel hostile are twice as likely to get injured as people who don't feel hostile. Men are more likely than women to get injured while angry.

Safety occurs in connection. For safety to hold, you will need to calm yourself and reconnect with yourself and then reconnect with your partner. Unless you and your partner reconnect as soon as possible after a train wreck, one or both partners can say and/or do a lot of damaging things in 24 hours.

If a solution does not lead to a reconnect, that means the story is not unpacked thoroughly or totally honestly, or more disconnects have occurred while unpacking the story (See Chapter Nine on Telling the Story). In this event, it is important to not pretend that a reconnect has happened. You will know in your body whether you have reconnected or whether you remain disconnected (See Chapter Thirteen on Finishing). If you remain disconnected, you must attend to those parts of the story that remain unpacked, or to parts of the story that have not been unpacked with total (caring) honesty or to parts of the unpacking that have created a disconnect for you. Stay with the process. Keep going until you feel reconnected.

Adaptations for Alpha-Alphas

An alpha-alpha pair may need to handle connection time differently than an alpha-beta pair. This has been Pat's experience in her relationships with several alpha partners, with her late husband Bill, and most recently, her sister, Mary, all of whom are also alphas.

> Mary and Pat recently took a month-long sailing trip together.They have a long history of getting along well together, but had never spent this much time together on a day-to-day basis. Many of their visits with each other had been times of recuperating together from crises of family illnesses and deaths. Occasionally, small disconnects had been swept under the rug.
>
> At the beginning of the trip, Pat requested that she and Mary not sweep issues under the rug and agree on guidelines they would use in handling the normal "glitches" that occur when living together on a day-to-day basis. This was especially important on a sailboat, where safety can depend on working together as a team. Since Pat has been using the guidelines outlined in this book, she requested that Mary read the book and consider using it, or some mutually agreeable variation, as their "roadmap" in handling problems that might arise between the two of them. Mary agreed. They made an initial agreement not to engage in any discussions about interpersonal difficulties if either of them had had alcohol to drink.
>
> Unfortunately, a difficulty arose before Mary had finished reading the book. Following their agreement, they sat and processed the difficulty before going to dinner at a special restaurant that they had chosen for their last night in this particular town. They felt good about their processing, and each stated that they felt finished.
>
> Later, after each had had a glass of wine at the restaurant, Mary brought up a topic she perceived to be incidental to their afternoon process. It seemed innocuous enough, so Pat responded, thinking that they were just going to be mellow and laugh and celebrate getting through their touchy time. Then Mary had something to say. Then Pat had something to say back. Before long, the conversation was getting heated. Mary, not yet having read the part about negotiating "time-outs," abruptly left the table while Pat was talking, going outside on the patio to cool down.
>
> Pat experienced Mary's leaving as a disconnect. She felt abandoned, and in response, whooshed to Powerland, immersed in the shame of being abandoned. While every bone in her body knew she shouldn't, she quietly paid the bill and left the restaurant. (She needs more practice in staying in the shame moment.)

Mary returned to the boat, enraged with Pat for leaving. She packed her overnight bag and left the boat. (At this point, you could say that two alphas were engaged in a pissing contest to see who could abandon whom the biggest. Obviously, there are no winners here.)

Each spent some time "cooling down," moving from righteous anger to shame and regret about their behavior. Each spent a tortured night, wondering how the other was, and if they would repair their relationship. They had never fought like this before.

By the time Mary called Pat the next morning, each had softened, but were yet too tender to talk about the fight. They sat down over a cup of coffee and contemplated how they would handle their situation. Without ignoring that they needed to talk, they decided that they needed to reconnect through doing things they enjoyed and did together well. They needed to bathe in their love in order to feel safe enough to process their fight. After all, each was fearful that the other would leave.

They aborted their previous plans to set sail that morning. They went to brunch at a nice restaurant, visited a museum, played with the dog, and laughed together. They never forgot that they needed to talk. But first they needed to reunite as a team, so they together could address the fight on their mutually held computer screen.

It took Mary a week to finish reading the book. In three talks (of one to two hours) over the ensuing two weeks, they processed their fight and the events leading up to it. They returned from the trip feeling more known, and knowing and loving each other more deeply.

While Mary and Pat are sisters and not a couple, the problems encountered in intimacy on a day-to-day basis between two alphas apply. We tell the story here because Pat's experience in alpha-alpha pairings is that in these pairings, as long as harm is not done within the 24 hour period after an anger flare-up, alpha-alpha pairs may well need to establish reconnection before talking, while alpha-beta pairs may need to talk more quickly, in order to establish reconnection. In both situations, anxiety may be the driver.

In alpha-alpha pairings, the anxiety may be about establishing safety first, through reconnection, to lessen the fear, either of what you may do to the other or what they may do to you. By spending the day together, Pat and Mary gained needed reassurance that they were not going to be left; then they could proceed to address the train wreck. Each alpha may need a time of self-soothing and reconnection before they are "fit for human consumption." In an alpha-beta pairing, the anxiety, especially for the beta, may be that the reconnect will not happen, so talking as soon as possible is better. In short, some couples may need to talk in order to reconnect, and some couples may need to go off separately and self-soothe or engage in reconnecting non-crisis-solving mutual

behavior long enough to calm down so that they can reconnect in order to talk.
In this example, alcohol clearly played a role in each sister's *Whoosh!* to Powerland. Alcohol and other disinhibiting substances can make us more vulnerable to a quick flight to Powerland. You may need an agreement to flag disconnects when consuming alcohol and deal with them later when no alcohol is being consumed. If this works, fine. If it doesn't work, your relationship is more important than alcohol. Stop drinking.

The Commitment

In either case, the reconnect is about a commitment to deal with train wrecks as soon as possible, and to do so safely. This commitment to safely reconnect as soon as possible and come to a mutually agreeable resolution of the crisis is made in the absence of knowing:

- When a train wreck might happen
- Why a train wreck just happened
- What the train wreck is about
- How you are ever going to be able to understand the train wreck
- What you are going to do to resolve this crisis and prevent similar crises in the future.

That's quite a commitment! And it must be made. Acting "nice" is not enough.

Why? In our version of Loveland, continuous connection is the first priority. Therefore any break in connection experienced by either participant is a crisis. If one partner experiences a disconnect, there is a disconnect. It is crazy-making to say to your partner, who reports a disconnect, "No, we're not disconnected."

We often avoid reporting an experienced disconnect on the basis of "not rocking the boat," or "maintaining peace," or niceness. We avoid on the basis of anticipating feeling shame at the possibility of being seen as a poor sport, spoiler, or troublemaker. We can avoid out of fear of being seen as unfair or picky or a whiner. We can avoid out of feelings of anger at having to be the one who "always" initiates, or out of feelings of doubt (without mutual exploration) about the rightness and clarity of our experience. And sometimes we avoid out of weariness. If the partner who experiences the break in connection avoids reporting and addressing a disconnect, then the relationship begins to hollow out and shrink in vibrance and aliveness and the pair increasingly descend into "role playing."

It is critical that if you are the partner experiencing the disconnect you soothe yourself (See Chapter Fifteen) and then call a crisis. Then you do whatever you need to do to maximize the probability of healing the connection through your intervention. Your intervention is calling a crisis and then arranging to reestablish the connection through talking. Things you might do in order to help yourself maximize the probability of a successful reconnection include journaling, consultation with trusted supporters of the relationship, then engaging with your partner in carefully dividing up of the problem and talk-times into manageable units, suitable timing, and venue choice.

The crisis has happened, and through poor management has become a train wreck. The damaging processes driven by fear, anger, defensiveness, and paranoia must be stopped. The participants must soothe themselves and calm down. The damage must be assessed. In addition to your self-soothing, anything you can do to help your partner feel safe in re-engaging with you will be helpful. Indicating your love, optimism about the relationship, expressing eagerness to "own" your part of the disconnect, and to understand your partner and properly deal with the disconnect are all useful. You can offer appropriate apologies, reassurance, and reminders (for both yourself and your partner) of your commitment to talk this through to a positive conclusion without knowing what it is going to require in time or effort.

This is not the time to go to the carnival, eat hot dogs, go about the housework, or otherwise pretend that nothing has happened. The recommitment to work through the Oh Shit! experience is mutually made. Other things such as fun, romance, sex, household tasks are not to go on as if nothing has happened. Faking normal in the face of a crisis that has evolved into a train wreck dooms your relationship to a chronic hollow shell. The hollow, chronically empty relationship may be something to present to the public under difficult (hopefully temporary) circumstances, but it is not something that a person can live in. Hollowness that is not attended to tends to be maintained. If you are not going to deal with a crisis when you are in the midst of it, when the hell are you going to deal with it?! Probably never. "Fakiness" is a habit. We may be still attached to and dependent upon our partner, but the love energy, the "juice" is gone. This state we call Chronic Marriage.

People in the state of Chronic Marriage go about their day with fake smiles on their faces. They may well be upstanding members of the community. They may do their work and maintain their households and cook together for church suppers, with cooperation. But there is no juice. They stay in the role of looking married, acting married, but are not really connected with themselves or with each other.

So, are you Chronically Married, or are you in Loveland? To have a commitment to deal with disconnects as soon as possible is not only respectful to ourselves, each other, and the relationship; it is also respectful to the other people in the Loveland web. When we as a couple are in a disconnect, we are likely to expose others we love to toxic spill off, either by exposing them to our fakiness, or by exposing them to our Powerland committee member's behavior and our unaddressed anger. When we take care of ourselves at the time of a disconnect we also take others we love out of harm's way. People in Loveland know when a couple is disconnected and fakiness is present.

> Joy recently asked her friend, Belinda, if she could come watch the Olympics with her. "No," replied Belinda. "My husband and I are strained with each other right now, and I won't put him in a situation in which he has to smile and pretend that everything is okay." Joy appreciated Belinda's stance, because it kept her from enduring an evening of fakiness.

People fake because of laziness, fear, ignorance of consequences, and/or because they learned their relationship skills from poor role models. Fear is understandable. You have committed to leave the familiar shore of Powerland, to share your truth in an unhurtful way, to listen with connected curiosity to your partner, and you have no idea how it is going to turn out with *each and every crisis*. To commit to this process always requires courage because there are no answers in advance. It helps to remember that even the bravest soldiers are not without fear. In the book *Flags of Our Fathers* (Bradley and Powers, 2000), the true story about the marines who took Iwo Jima in World War II, many marines reported anxiety, even to the point of diarrhea, while on the ship headed for their destiny.

Like the marines who invaded Iwo Jima, alphas' warriors are very courageous, and are usually quite focused in a fearless way during battle. Once in action, alphas have fearless courage. Anxiety usually happens only during the initial, "who will blink first" moment. Every alpha knows that in Powerland, blinking first often results in an unfavorable outcome.

Also like the Iwo Jima marines, some alphas can experience fear prior to initiation, especially if they are the one about to initiate. They can also experience fear at the onset of real risk. In the periods prior to the onset of announcing a disconnect and initiating repair, or prior to the onset of a discussion involving risky activity (such as talking from the heart rather than from Powerland), or involving real risk of shame or risk to the relationship, some alphas can experience extreme fear and anxiety. This is the moment that requires courage in the face of fear. The fear may be about initiating, or it may be about information and feelings we anticipate receiving from our partner. This is especially true if we do not feel skillful or knowledgeable in dealing with the risk we are about to take.

The fear becomes even more extreme if the stakes are high and the skill is low. Therefore, before we initiate or accept participation in a crisis discussion, we are required to use our courage in the face of fear to allow our coach to be in charge in the discussion; we are required to use our courage to do the right thing (like a good marine). Every soldier, firefighter, and policeman knows that coming to grips with fear, rather than denying it, helps them keep a cool head and handle their weapons better in the anticipated situation. Courage is not about fearlessness. Rather, real courage is defined as moving forward in the face of fear. It takes courage to say, "We have a problem; we need to talk, we need to figure out what the problem is and what to do about it."

While in Powerland, we experience anxiety about blinking first. But in Loveland, confessing and sharing that we are suddenly anxious and that it is hard to stay in the conversation makes us more loveable and is much more likely to elicit a helpful response from our partner (unless our partner is driven by a Mean Gene/Warrior III, who will exploit our vulnerability). In Loveland, do not worry; if you falter, just be honest about it.

Having courage and taking the risk, in these situations where malice is absent, is different from being vulnerable in a climate that is clearly not trustable, or in a situation in which your partner is in Powerland rage or being emotionally abusive. In these situations, safety must be established first. This can be done by interrupting your partner's behavior or announcing that you are going to leave until he is able to soothe himself and be safely available to talk. Learn more about this in the following chapter, which has to do with establishing boundaries.

In Pat and Marty's experience, different alphas get anxious in response to different specific circumstances. Marty becomes anxious when he believes he is about to discover that he has unnecessarily hurt someone. It takes courage for him to begin to listen to the other person's story, which he fears will include information about how he has hurt someone and didn't know it. His worst case is having done a positive act to please, and discovering that it was taken negatively for spurious reasons that are amenable neither to correction nor apology.

Pat gets anxious when she experiences hurt in response to another's actions. She worries that she is being too picky, too difficult. What motivates Pat to have courage in a crisis situation is the knowledge of how bad she will feel if she doesn't use all available skills to address the problem. "I may feel afraid that I will be unskillful; I may be afraid that I won't manage my committee well and that I will be embarrassed about that; I may be afraid my partner will try to overpower me; I may be afraid of not knowing the outcome. But *not* dealing with it always comes back to bite me in the butt, in ten minutes or ten weeks. Not dealing with it pushes me farther down a road of living in a fake relationship or farther up the hill toward living alone in Powerland."

Laziness is guaranteed to produce repetitive undesirable results. What is laziness in this context? It is your choice to fearfully avoid the possibility of doing your best and failing anyhow. It is the stupid and false belief that you can avoid blame for a bad outcome by not courageously initiating your best effort. More importantly, it is also a sense of entitlement that you should not have to initiate and take the risk of experiencing and speaking of the humiliation of being disconnected. It is about cowardice and the belief that your partner should take care of you, rather than your doing your part, the very hard part of managing your fear, stepping up to the bar and addressing the disconnect.

It is the authors' experience that when malice has not been present, all the failures to date in using this material have resulted from at least one of the partners placing *something else* as a higher priority than continuous connection. Something else might be niceness, safety, peace, or any of the other things we've addressed here. An example of having a higher priority than continuous connection is a couple Marty knows in which one partner burns so brightly on behalf of a passionate humanitarian cause that his pursuit has become a higher priority than continuous connection with his partner. He depletes all the psychic oxygen in the relationship by talking constantly about his project, leaving little or no conversational space for his partner. His interruptive boundary violations (such as barging in on his partner while she is showering to ask her advice on a burning question) become "routine" in the frantic effort to "get on with the project." Solitude has become too scarce for them. In their case, *"doing good"* is getting *bad*! Intervention through the processes we are describing to mutually manage competing priorities is now a dire necessity. Otherwise, one or both of the partners will experience burnout. "Burnt people crisps" do not make good lovers.

If fake safety is made a higher priority than continuous connection, it is important to remember that real safety is established by doing what you need to do to get back to Loveland. When you address disconnects as soon as possible, you are being respectful of yourself, of each other, the relationship, and the situation. You are being respectful of those around you.

This is a matter of principle, or character. Our inner coach, relentlessly following a small number of the carefully chosen guidelines that we are presenting here, can rein in the single-mindedness of the other internal committee members. Otherwise, these members will destroy connection by insisting on their solitary mantras as higher priorities than continuous connection.

You are moving *away* from a situation of doing potentially unsafe things, and back *toward* the safety of Loveland. If you started this book ignorant of any of the principles and practices we have described, you now no longer have that excuse. Practice, practice, practice!

Imagine this: You are dealing with a disconnect. Your advance commitment to an absence of malice means that even in the face of a disconnect/train wreck, there will be no abuse, no sense of unsafety and/or humiliation of either party. If you abuse your partner or allow yourself to be abused, if you trick or exploit each other, that is bad. You will fail to resolve the crisis. How do you ensure good behavior from both partners? This is where boundaries come in, our next exploration.

CHAPTER EIGHT

BOUNDARIES

By definition, a boundary is something that marks the limits; it is the dividing line. On either side of the line is something else. In this case, on one side would be safe Loveland behaviors, and on the other would be unsafe Powerland behaviors. The boundary is the threshold between these two quite different lands. A swamp is a river without banks. Boundaries, like the clear, defined sides of a river, make events flow clean and clear; they make it possible for our boat to navigate its way through Loveland. Without the sides of the river, water spreads across the land and becomes a swamp. Without boundaries, instead of progressing through Loveland, we find ourselves bogged down in the swamps of Powerland. In the following pages we are going to address some of the common areas in which couples need to set and/or negotiate boundaries.

Name Calling

Boundaries help us negotiate our own and our partner's safety. One way to do this is to agree that there will be no name-calling. Names that are sometimes used and are important to eliminate include bitch, bastard, creep, and asshole. There should also be an agreed-upon boundary around character defamation. Character defamations are words that undermine the self of the other, for example, calling our partner a sneaky, lazy or irresponsible person would be character defamation. Saying instead something like, "I'm wondering why you didn't tell me the whole story about that situation" would be a more respectful way of communicating.

Defining the Problem

Sometimes boundaries need to be set about how the problem is defined. Here is one couple's story.

> Maurice and Sally visited an eastern European country for an extended period. Sally had frequented one of the shops nearby their villa and had become quite friendly with the shopkeepers, a loving husband and wife. As time for their return to the states approached, the shopkeepers told Maurice that they had a special gift for Sally, a bottle of their homemade native wine. They asked Maurice to bring Sally to their shop the Saturday night prior to their departure so that they could share a drink of wine with them before presenting Sally with the bottle.
>
> Maurice and Sally ate their dinner at home that night, and Sally delighted in anticipation of a glass of the wine after dinner. When they arrived at the shop, the shopkeepers were very happy to see them, and excitedly presented them with the homemade wine, bottled, as was the custom in this somewhat poor country, in a glass water bottle. The shopkeepers were slightly embarrassed that they had forgotten to bring glasses, but gave Sally and Maurice each a sip from the aluminum lid of the bottle. As they finished their sip, the shop became very busy. The shopkeepers beckoned them to wait, so they did.
>
> Seated on a wall in the open-air shop, Sally and Maurice enjoyed watching the Saturday night festivities at this seaside resort. People walked by in beautiful native clothing, chatting and laughing. Time went by, and Sally fell into the gaiety of the evening as the shop remained busy and the shopkeepers naturally preoccupied. Sally remembered her anticipation of the glass of wine, a good dessert wine. Upon giving it some thought, she decided to take a sip out of the bottle. After all, the shopkeepers had gifted it to her, it was alcohol, which would kill germs, and if her partner wanted some, it would not be the first time they shared germs! It was Saturday night and a party atmosphere prevailed. She picked up the bottle and took a sip.
>
> Her joy was shattered when Maurice spoke. "You are a drunk!" he proclaimed. "Only *drunks* drink out of the bottle!" He said this loudly

enough for everyone within a ten-foot radius to hear. Sally was mortified. And they were certainly disconnected. Maurice had grown up with an alcoholic grandfather, of whom he had been quite ashamed as a boy, so Sally understood the fear, shame and humiliation underlying such a Powerland exclamation. That did not lessen her chagrin in the moment.

Later, when they arrived back at their vacation home, Maurice began a discussion with, "I am very disappointed with your public drunken behavior." Setting boundaries for her own safety as well as that of the relationship, Sally replied with, "The way that you are defining this problem is so off-putting to me that I can not enter that discussion."

Here are some useful variations of that statement:

I need for both of us to define the problem together in a way that doesn't make me feel like a bad person. I did what I did without malice.

Your further abuse of me is worsening our train wreck. Stop.

The way you are defining this problem is so deleterious to my feeling halfway decent about myself that I need for you not to do that.

In order to proceed with this discussion, I need for you, or us, to define the problem in a different way.

Time-outs

To maintain safety, another boundary may need to be set around time-outs. When we know enough about our self to know that we are capable of getting "hot," losing our temper, and losing control of our warrior, it is also a good idea to put some boundary around our warrior prior to discussing the problem. One simple way to do this is to agree that when either partner recognizes himself or herself or the other heating up or about to move farther up the hill into Powerland, they will identify that fact, either through a sign, an inquiry or a statement. One useful signal is the "Time-out" signal, with two hands perpendicular to each other. At that point, a time-out can happen until the potentially "hot" partner is reestablished in his or her commitment to get back to Loveland.

Time-outs and other boundaries are important if your partner slips into abusive Powerland behavior and does not recognize it. If you are on the receiving end of abuse, that is not the time to be open-hearted. Neither is it the time to fly to Powerland yourself. Curiosity expressed to your partner may help. You might ask, in a kind inquiring voice, something like, "What is going on, that you would speak to me like that?" If your partner persists in Powerland activities, firm boundaries need to be set around engaging in anything until your partner has stopped abusive Powerland language and behavior. You might say something like, "Please stop talking to me like that," or "I'm removing myself from the room until you stop talking to me like that. Let me know when you are available."

Time

Other boundary setting may need to occur about the issue of time itself. Hopefully, you will have time to resolve the crisis in one sitting and within a period of time that is tolerable to each of you. However, women and/or betas often have more tolerance and patience than do men and/or alphas when it comes to boundary-setting discussions. They also are more readily willing to listen to their partner's story, with its associated emotions and relationship to their history, and to tell their own story and propose solutions in non-linear, indirect ways. Perhaps you have guests coming for dinner and you need to make a plan to disengage, with time to soothe and center yourselves, if necessary, before the guests arrive.

Here is a story from Pat and Bill's marriage.

> Bill was an innately restless individual. He had a short attention span. His restlessness often served him well in his work as an attorney, where it was useful to get to the bottom of things quickly, though sometimes at work, he had to practice focusing his attention for longer periods of time. He loved Pat; he loved the adventure of their marriage, and was deeply committed to working things out. Being a therapist, and a woman, Pat had more experience with long process discussions. Initially, when they began discussing problems in their relationship, Bill tried to adopt Pat's natural tolerance for long discussions. She could sit and talk about things for hours on end (also known to Bill as hours *ad nauseum*), with a great deal of patience.
>
> Even Bill's office practice of focusing his attention and being patient in listening to others did not prepare him for the lengthy discussions when they had disconnects in their relationship. "How can she *do* this for so long?!" Bill thought, in exasperation one day, after several hours of processing. He noticed that he began to get cranky after about an hour and fifteen minutes. After several episodes of becoming cranky and noticing his temptation to slip to Powerland in his crankiness, Bill finally suggested that he take a half hour break after an hour of discussion, during which he would take a walk. Bill and Pat agreed that if they needed more time after the second hour, they would schedule

time later that day, or if that weren't possible, the next day. Bill began to relax more in the beginning of their discussions, knowing that he wasn't likely to become fidgety. The periods in between their talk times gave each of them time to reflect on what the other said, and on creative ways to avoid the next related disconnect.

Boundaries Related to Optional Behavioral Choices

Some boundaries need to be absolute. John Gottman, in his groundbreaking research on the causes of divorce, names four clear causes of relationship destruction. He calls these the Four Horsemen of the Apocalypse (Gottman, 1999, pp.27-34). They are:

1. Criticism: Unsolicited criticism, especially if it focuses on the person rather than on a specific alterable behavior.

2. Defensiveness. Guys, every good defense is offensive. When we become defensive with our partner, it appears to our partner that we believe she or he acted in malice. We come across like we think our partner is mean and must be guarded against. We come across like we don't trust our partner, or like we are being sneaky and have something to hide, or like a coward.

3. Contempt. Since the shame associated with the Oh Shit!! moment is specifically where the disconnect occurs, contempt from one's partner intensely exaggerates that shame. Further, if the contemptuous behavior continues after the Oh Shit! moment, any healing discussion becomes impossible. Only physical abuse is worse than shaming behavior in destroying relationships.

4. Stonewalling. Warrior I will stonewall from a "suck-it-up and-say-nothing," motto. This is often because he doesn't know what else to do, is flooded with feelings and thoughts (and can't sort them out), and can't speak or hear any new information. If the Secret Agent initiates the stonewalling, it is a clever ruse to frustrate your partner to death. The Secret Agent knows that by stonewalling, he appears innocent, cannot be quoted, observers will see him as longsuffering, and he creates the illusion that the problem is solely that of his partner. If his partner would only calm down, everything would be fine. Stonewalling is the elephant in the living room covered with the cloak of invisibility; it still gets in the way—you're going to stumble on it.

We add a fifth horseman:

5. Physical or verbal abuse.

If either partner endures any of the above, but chooses to preserve the marriage, they end up in a stable but unhappy marriage, which we previously termed "Chronic Marriage". They put up with each other, joylessly.

Boundaries to prevent the above behaviors are absolutely mandatory. This includes, for example, maintaining moderation of alcohol intake, of overwork/fatigue and of distracting over-commitments, all of which produce toxic states that make it more likely that the warriors, whichever ones are present, will run amuck and do one or more of the above hurtful behaviors.

However, life's pains do not always come in such large, disastrous packages. Sometimes one's behavior is merely annoying, frustrating, impeding, thwarting, or less than desirable. These behaviors also require addressing.

Voluntary Behaviors

Voluntary behaviors for which there is more than one choice can be shaped by boundaries to prevent poor results. In a partnership, when it is clear from experience that you have more than one choice in a given situation, you can learn to cooperate with one another in a variety of circumstances through all seasons of the relationship. Here is an example from Pat and Bill's experience:

> To both Bill and Pat, keeping their word and honoring their commitments, large or small, was important, as it should be to all couples. When they were cruising on their sailboat, Pat's job was to empty the trash. One particular day had been long, hot, and hard. They had a disagreement about their docking procedure as they came into harbor that night. A fight ensued. Pat stalked away, grabbed the garbage off the boat, and proceeded toward an unlit area outside the gates of the marina, known to be in an unsafe area of the town. Bill pleaded with her not to go, but Pat's Powerland Soldier was now in the driver's seat. She retorted, "It's my job, and I'm going to do it!"
>
> As she navigated her way through the unlit, unsafe area to empty the trash, Pat felt fearful and also had time to reflect on her shameful behavior. Upon dumping the trash, she turned and her heart softened as she saw her tired but loving husband, who had protectively followed her, despite his anger and fatigue, to make sure she was safe. They hugged, and over scrambled eggs and candlelight, set a boundary around discussing hot topics after stressful sailing days. They agreed to reconnect and to earmark the need for a discussion, to happen after

they were sufficiently rested. They discussed ways to minimize stressful sailing days. Pat agreed not to allow her commitment to keep her word to be used spitefully or to compromise her safety.

A voluntary behavior that is acceptable in one season of the relationship may need to be altered in a different season:

> Marty has a chronic, incurable, and ultimately fatal cancer. Treatment can sometimes be physically weakening. One of his jobs in his marriage was to do the household shopping at Costco. Recently, he encountered a limit in his ability to do this alone; the act of shopping, loading the goods, and driving home exhausted him. He called his wife Leslie on the cell phone on the way home and said he was on the way with a full truck and an emergency need for her to do all the unloading. By the time Marty reached home, he was physically unable to unload the truck. Leslie, who had a flu and wasn't feeling well herself, was left with the unexpected task of unloading the truck by herself. A disconnect occurred. After Marty rested, they discussed new shopping options appropriate to this season of their marriage. Marty agreed that when he felt the need to fill the truck at Costco, he would either bring his son along or pay an able-bodied teenage neighbor to come along to help with the loading and unloading.

In both of these situations, there were two kinds of bad behavior around keeping one's word. Under *almost* all circumstances, not keeping your word is an immediate crisis. In Bill and Pat's situation, Pat kept her word, adding to a crisis because she did so in malice. In Marty and Leslie's situation, Marty kept his word in light of his newly occurring and previously undiscovered limitations. This became a painful, disruptive overextension, leading to a crisis of disconnection. Alphas often overextend themselves out of arrogance ("Of course, I'm exhausted, but I'm bigger than life, and will do the job anyway."). Betas often keep their word when it is not useful to do so out of adaptation.

> George and Erica are an alpha-beta pair. George, the beta, was careful to keep his word with Erica, an alpha. He knew that she had often been let down by her alcoholic mother, who frequently broke her word when Erica was small, engendering much sadness and anger in Erica. It was George's day to pick up their daughter Ann from school. George, who had stayed home from work with a terrible cold, rather than call Erica to see if she might pick up Ann, dragged himself out of bed, picked up Ann, became light-headed on his drive home and skidded into a parked car. His excessive adapting precipitated a family crisis.

In the examples above, terms and boundaries need to be renegotiated as circumstances change. These changes are often first noted by crisis. These gifts of crises often alert the couple that renegotiations need to occur.

How Alpha-Alphas and Alpha-Betas Set Boundaries

Bill and Pat were an alpha-alpha pair. With work and experience, most of the time they successfully set boundaries around Powerland behaviors. Marty and Leslie are an alpha-beta pair, with Leslie being, in Marty's words, "a beta with a backbone of steel." Betas with backbones are generally good at defining and defending their boundaries without getting hateful about it. This is simply because betas have little or no capacity for malice.

Alphas can also learn to set boundaries without getting hateful once they decide to do it lovingly. It is here that the positive aspect of the inner Warrior, the Soldier, can be useful. The warrior can use all her/his strength to stop any other mean-spirited team member from abducting the coach's position. He can stand guard and assert that no hateful words will be spoken.

Betas without backbones have difficulty setting boundaries. If you are one of these, it may be important to find a way to learn to grow and stiffen your backbone. If you are partnered with an alpha, it is critical to learn to do this. If you know aspects of your relationship or discussions that need some boundaries but you haven't set them, these are good places to start practicing. Pick something small in the beginning, and work your way up to the more difficult issues. If you are unable to do this on your own, you might consider reading a book on assertiveness or you might consider counseling for learning these skills. Two good books are *Your Perfect Right* by Alberti and Emmons (2005), and *When I Say No I Feel Guilty* by Manuel Smith (1979).

> Pat is an introvert, and a psychotherapist. During her marriage to Bill, she was still working full-time. Her job required much focus in talking and listening to people. Typical of most introverts, she likes to mull things over inside before speaking about them. She is also a morning person, who turns into a pumpkin usually no later than 9:00 P.M. Bill was very extroverted and an attorney. He spent his workdays talking with people and, like all extroverts, was energized by this. He loved the challenge of intimate conversations with Pat and often gained insight by talking with her, even about problems or difficulties they encountered. Shortly after they were married and living together, Bill, in his inimitable way, wanted to discuss some difficulty they were encountering at 10:00 P.M. when they went to bed. (He wasn't really sleepy anyway, and the conversation would be interesting!) "Let's talk about something!" he would say, enthusiastically.

Pat loved Bill, wanted to be a good wife and, though exhausted from listening and working with people all day, had difficulty turning down Bill's requests for conversation. She found, however, that when she engaged with him at this time of night she often became short-tempered or was not able to really tell her story because she had not had time to think about it when she was fresh.

After several of these unsuccessful "pumpkin conversations," Pat knew she must set a boundary. She told Bill that she was no good at problem-solving conversations as part of bedtime pillow talk. Bill, as an alpha, consequently disliking not getting what he wanted and therefore needing to see if she *really* meant that, attempted another intimate problem-solving conversation several nights later. Pat, having rehearsed this possibility in her head, lovingly touched his cheek and said, "Honey, if we talk about this now, I will be no good and not helpful. In fact, if we talk about this now, I am fearful that Attila the Hun will show up! I will be glad to get up half an hour earlier tomorrow and discuss this with you when I am fresh. If that is not enough time, we can then determine another time that will work for both of us." Bill grinned, agreed to a morning appointment and kissed her goodnight.

Alphas who have grown up in abusive households also have difficulty setting boundaries. Growing up in these households they may have observed that assertion of boundaries led to some version of emotional (and sometimes physical!) harm or in the extreme, physical abuse, or even death. They become subordinate in a relationship with another alpha. If you are one of these, it is important to establish safety with your partner *before* an intense situation arises. You can share your history, and obtain reassurance from your partner that the consequences of your boundary-setting will be respectful ones.

Joe had grown up with an abusive father. Late one cold night when Joe was quite ill, his father entered his room and told him to empty the garbage. When Joe replied that he wouldn't right now but would in the morning, his father hit him on the side of his face.

Joe's wife, Linda, was an assertive alpha who often asked Joe to do household chores without noticing when he might be involved with something else. Joe began to feel resentful of Linda's requests. He spoke with a friend, who encouraged him to ask Linda how she would respond if he declined and postponed one of her requests. Reminding himself that unlike his father, Linda had never hit him or even threatened to hurt him, he worked up his courage to tell her how he felt when she asked him to do a household chore while he was busy. He asked her how it would be if he temporarily declined the chore and did it later.

Linda was surprised to learn the ways in which she had missed noticing Joe's involvement in some other activity. Together they made a list of household chores and who would do what, which gave Joe flexibility around when he did his share and relieved Linda of having to ask.

Exercise: Think of a situation in which you have difficulties setting a boundary. It might be about time parameters in problem-solving; it might be about the way your partner frames some problem. Write about the situation below and write some ideas you have for lovingly setting boundaries. Start with some easier situation, and then move to a more difficult situation.

At this point in the process, you have

1. Reminded yourself that you are a volunteer.
2. Reminded yourself of your commitment to an absence of malice. You have engaged the coach on your inner committee to take control of any Powerland committee members who might sabotage that commitment.
3. Committed to continuous connection.
4. Identified that a disconnect (a crisis) has happened.
5. Acted upon your commitment to deal with disconnects as soon as possible after they happen.
6. Set boundaries around any potential unsafe behaviors and conflicting time parameters or other commitments.

You are now ready to continue with the process. The next step is for each of you to tell your story and to listen to the other. This is the process of *unpacking* the train wreck. Unpacking refers to an extended discussion of the actual events surrounding the crisis and their meaning to each of the partners.

CHAPTER NINE

TELLING THE STORY

A disconnect, a crisis, a train wreck, or an "Oh Shit!" moment has happened. One or both partners have zoomed to Powerland. *If only one partner has whooshed to Powerland, or if only one partner is aware of a disconnect, the disconnect has still occurred.* The partner who has not taken the jet plane to Powerland is in the position of rowing his little boat over to Powerland to help bring them both back to Loveland. You agree that there is a disconnect. ***If only one partner perceives that there is a disconnect, the other partner must accept that there is.*** This is crucial; you must accept this. You must not try to fix a problem alone; it must be done mutually.

Solitary Solutions Suck

Do not examine the problem and propose solutions until a mutually agreed upon understanding of the disconnect can be confirmed. It is important to look at the sequence of events prior to the train wreck, in other words, how it happened. You can't do this alone. You can't figure it out all by yourself and then decide on a solution and go about practicing it, announced or unannounced. Solitary solutions suck. If you want a deep and lasting solution to whatever caused the crisis, you must work *together* with your partner to arrive at a workable solution. You *must* do this together. You cannot solve the problem without cooperation and discussion with your partner. This is especially true because the first solution is experimental and may not work well enough to suit both of you. Therefore, the solution may need to be reworked.

Have you ever been in the situation in which, without talking to the other person about the problem, you make an announcement of something you or they are going to do to solve the problem? You expect great appreciation and what you get instead is just the opposite of appreciation. Right? That is because no problem between partners can be solved without input from both partners.

Why will these things happen? Because without your partner's input, you are not going to understand the problem sufficiently well to address it in a way that really works. You will get tired and resentful.

Solitary solutions suck, because in attempting them, one or more of the typical failures are inevitable.

1. Your solution is fitted to the wrong problem, not the one your partner perceives. Then you're going to hear your partner saying, "That's not the problem!"

> Jessica comes to bed exhausted because Robert watches sports on television while she gets their two children ready for bed, packs lunches for the following day, and washes the dishes. She wishes that Robert would volunteer to help her with these tasks. She has been "too tired" for sex. Robert says, "Honey, I know you are tired when you come to bed at night; don't worry. We can wake up an hour earlier in the morning and have sex then!" He doesn't understand why Jessica starts sleeping in the guest bedroom.

2. Your solution will be warped and useless because it excludes some information that only your partner has.

> Each year, Hugh and Pam have routinely taken a week exclusively for themselves at a ski resort. Pam feels reluctant to leave their two teenage sons at home unattended this year; one of them has been sneaking out after hours. Hugh notices Pam's reluctance (without knowing the reason) and decides that Pam is bored with skiing. He comes home and enthusiastically announces that this year, he has booked a flight to Hawaii instead of to the ski resort. He can't understand the look of horror on Pam's face.

3. It is a fine solution for someone else, but it is not acceptable to your partner.

> Buzz and Dolly want to re-ignite the romance they experienced in the early days of their marriage. In a "boy's night out" Buzz's friend Tim shares that he and his wife Alice have had passionate nights after watching erotic movies. Buzz brings home an armload of pornographic films. Dolly, brought up in a conservative environment, is disgusted.

4. Even worse yet, if you tend to be an over-adaptive person (pleaser, accommodator, self-compromiser, suck-up), you are going to give away more than you need to in your proposed solution.

> Ken, like most of us, doesn't like to be criticized. His wife, Joan, is very critical. (Criticism is another Powerland move; it is an attempt to have it our way through making the other feel bad.) One day, Ken had enough and blew up at Joan after yet another aggressively critical remark from her. A disconnect occurred. Joan, hurt by Ken's angry outburst, became silent and would not speak to him. Ken, in an attempt to reconnect, promised that he would never lash back at Joan when she criticized him.
>
> This is an example of giving away too much. What Ken could have more usefully said is, "What just happened? Why, under this or any other circumstance, would you think that criticism of me is a valid response?" This statement invites a reconnect, implicitly sets a boundary, and sets the stage for a dialogue to address the problem from both sides. It also prevents Ken from making a promise that would be difficult to keep, because Ken's promise does nothing to address Joan's criticizing.

As you can see, guys, the perceived problem is only the tip of the iceberg of problems that would have emerged had you talked about it with your partner. This iceberg will sink the ship of your proposed solution. So, you must solve the problem together; you must come up with a mutually agreeable solution. In order to do this, you must each tell your story, safely.

Establish Safety

Make yourselves safe, and do what you can do to optimize a reconnect. It is critical to soothe yourself, if necessary (See Chapter Fifteen). Use journaling, or consult with someone you trust to support your relationship. It is very important to do this before calling a crisis/disconnect.

Another aspect of safety is to pick a suitable place and sufficient time, when you are relatively certain to have the right energy, interest, and calmness. Indicate your love, your optimism about the relationship, your eagerness to learn about your part in the problem, and to know your partner better. Reassure your partner of your awareness of their absence of malice. Or, if there has been malice on their part, and you have demanded they cease and desist their malicious behavior, reassure them of your belief in their return to Loveland and help them soothe themselves through their Oh Shit! moment.

If you are the one who has declared the crisis, reassure your partner of your desire to understand them through connected curiosity (more about this soon). Let your partner know that you are more interested in initially understanding them than their "getting" your perspective right away, since you have had much more time to mull it over and identify your own point of view.

In establishing safety, it is also important to carefully parse out the problem. Parsing out a problem occurs when both partners describe to themselves and each other the "problem" in congruent words and mappings. (See "My Trip to Deadwood" in the Epilogue at the end of this book.)

As partners, you must have a commitment to use your power together, in the service of love, to get your boat back to Loveland. You have identified the disconnect, marshaled that commitment, set aside time, done what you need to do to make yourself and the other safe from malice, and negotiated any related boundaries. Now the exploration itself begins; it is time to unpack the event, to tell your stories.

How We Tell Our Story

How we tell our story to our partner is very important. We should never tell our own story in a way that is deliberately hurtful to our partner. For example, "I felt like you drove a stake through my heart when you did that," (this is the Horseman of Severe Criticism) or, "You looked like a slut to me at the party" (Horseman of Severe Criticism plus Contempt). When we say things like this, we can be sure that one of our Powerland committee members is speaking. The message we are sending to our partner when we do this is "You have hurt me with what you did (victim stance) and I want you to feel pain now (persecutor stance)." In addition we are setting them up to become the rescuer by secretly hoping that they will apologize and make nice to us to assuage our rage and pain.

With our best intentions, while maintaining an absence of malice, in partnership, we take turns telling our story, looking together at the events that unfolded that preceded the disconnect. One partner can speak while the other listens, and then change places. It is also okay if one starts and the other chimes in, as long as the chime-ins are in the service of making things clearer or communicating understanding. Decide which way works for you. Angry, blaming chime-ins will not help.

Respecting Boundaries

You must be respectful of your partner's boundaries even though their requirements around their space or time or circumstance may be an inconvenience to you. You wish that they did not have those requirements; that happens. Even with their best efforts your partner may not be able to give anything near what you want. Expecting, accepting, and working with differences and limitations (boundaries) that your partner sets is part of the patina of having a real person for a partner.

I-Statements

You must begin the discussion with the intention NOT to be in the power place. When both people are truly committed to non-malicious interactions, to holding back any malice, and to using "I-statements", you will move the discussion along more productively. You will be more likely to be viewed as non-malicious if you take personal responsibility for your own perceptions, thoughts about your part of the problem, and your feelings by using "I-statements."

What is an "I-statement"? An I-Statement is a sentence which begins with the word "I" and then moves on to claim some portion of the problem that you own, including your own perceptions, thoughts, feelings, and interests presented honestly and non-maliciously. Here are some examples:

> "When you were talking with that beautiful woman at the party for what seemed to me like a very long time, I felt ignored, and I felt threatened. I especially felt that way when you were still talking with her twenty minutes beyond the time upon which we had agreed to leave. It was hard not to think that I am unimportant to you. I didn't take very good care of myself; instead of joining you, or asking you if you were ready to go, I withered inside, waiting for you to remember."

> "I had an expectation that you would call me if you were going to be late. I'm wondering if you share that expectation."

> "I really wanted you to call me more when you were out of town."

A "you-statement," on the other hand, is just that: it speaks about the other, not about ourselves. Here are the same examples from above, but re-phrased into "you-statements":

> "You talked with that beautiful woman for a long time, ignoring me and *making me* (notice the drama triangle position of victim) feel threatened. You forgot about the time upon which we had agreed to leave. I wasn't important to you. You didn't take good care of me."
>
> "You didn't call me when you were going to be late and you left me in a damned lurch!"
>
> "You didn't call me very much when you were out of town. You went into a damned silent zone, and I didn't know what was going on. Are you seeing someone else?"

As you read the "I-statements" and then the "you-statements," do you respond differently inside to one or the other? We tend to feel more empathetic with the person who is speaking when they use "I-statements." We tend to feel more defensive or offended and *act* offensive when the speaker uses "you-statements." Every defense is an offense, because you have defined the other person as attacking you. They, in turn, will experience a "you-statement" response as a counterattack, which will then lock you both into fighting and Powerland. Every such relationship argument is an exercise in foolishness in which each person serves as their own lawyer in a courtroom with no judge, no jury and no agreed-upon civil procedure.

When we speak from the "I-statement" place, we generally feel more empowered in the service of love, because we are speaking from the center of our own truth. We feel better about ourselves, because we are speaking our truth without attacking the other, and in Loveland, it doesn't feel good to attack someone else. We leave space for our partner to have their own story. In this way, the unpacking process can be done as a team, with room for both players.

When we speak with "you-statements," we can easily fall into a victim stance, for example, "*You* make me feel...." We make it more difficult for our partner to tell their story, and therefore for us to problem-solve together, because we haven't left them space, and we haven't really given ourselves space.

The "I-statement" was invented in order to prevent communication problems. If it is used correctly and with the right motivation, it will work. It will *not* work, even if used correctly, if you are still trying to get power *over* your partner.

One good way to check yourself to see if you are using the "I-stance" correctly and with good motivation is to ask yourself the following question before using it: "What is my intention in saying this?" If your intention is to somehow hurt your partner (often done because you want them to hurt in the same way that you are hurting) or intimidate them into doing something you want that they don't want, you are using an "I-statement" in a way that undermines getting you and your partner back to Loveland. Here are examples of "I-statements" that are Powerland "I-statements":

> "I just may walk out of here some day."
>
> "I wouldn't talk like that to me if I were you."
>
> "I don't want to hear your story."
>
> "I could hurt somebody at a time like this."

Give Your Storytelling Enough Time

Sometimes telling the story takes time because our differences come from different cultural backgrounds. When Leslie and Marty came together to "unpack" one of their problems (more later), it became clear to them that the differences in their different childhood cultural backgrounds were significant to consider.

> Marty and Leslie dated for one year before deciding to build a home and live together. Marty was fifty-two years old, Leslie was forty-six years old, and each had been previously divorced. After their divorces, they had each spent several years alone, contemplating what they wanted in a relationship and thinking about their own second chance. They worked out many things before moving in together and had established a great deal of trust in themselves and the relationship. They each worked and had separate interests, took trips together and separately, and enjoyed their date nights, each Wednesday and weekends. All times, including bedtime, were coordinated. What Marty didn't know is that while they were dating, Leslie had used afternoon naps in order to be able to stay up late on Friday and Saturday nights. On Wednesday nights, they went to bed together at 9:00 P.M. (her schedule) after a leisurely dinner. The trouble came unexpectedly when they moved in together.
>
> Leslie grew up in a quiet suburb in Minneapolis, the eldest in a family of five children. Her mother ran the household, caringly and carefully, using a variety of rituals and techniques to prevent chaos. One of the rituals was that at 9:00 p.m., everyone had to settle down for a 9:30 p.m. bedtime. Days began early. This routine brought Leslie great peace. Some of her most comforting memories from her childhood were those of finishing a day well and settling down for her regular bedtime. This

bedtime gave her an "all's right with the world" feeling. Additionally, her biological clock, her Circadian rhythm, had adjusted to this very regular comforting bedtime. It brought her to her workday well-rested and refreshed.

Marty grew up in Manhattan. He is very bright and enjoys intellectual stimulation. His sleeping and waking matched the city's tempo. His most awake and energized time of the day began around 10:00 P.M. His parents were somewhat in awe of his intellect and the related academic achievements he had earned, so they allowed him to stay up as late as he wished from an early age. Before he and Leslie moved in together, on the nights that weren't date nights he was often up reading, studying, or preparing lectures until the wee hours of the morning. He enjoyed his late-night world.

After moving in together, because 9:30 bedtime was so important to Leslie, Marty initially came to bed with her. However, as his late-night engine kicked in, he became enlivened. His energy increased as the hours went by. The man's funny! He wants to entertain! Leslie was his only audience. This was not good. Sometimes he would get on his computer and write ideas that came to him, and would want to share these with Leslie and get her feedback and appreciation for their brilliance. He told funny stories or began conversations that he thought were fascinating and was sure Leslie would find them to be also. Leslie's sleep schedule was severely disrupted. She went into her workdays feeling insufficiently rested. (Sleep deprivation is a frequently occurring, and often unmentioned, problem for couples who live together.)

As they began more serious discussions about this problem, they each talked more about their cultural background; each gained a heretofore missed understanding of the other's different cultural background. This became a pivotal point in moving toward a solution to this problem.

Stay tuned; we will finish this story later so that you will see how good the solution is, even if it took eighteen months of painfully persistent effort.

Telling our stories might involve telling about childhood events, happy or traumatic, that influenced our response in a situation. Both Leslie and Marty had childhood joy in their differing bedtime routines. Even happy childhood events that strongly influence your adult habits can be problematic for your partner. Roger and Nancy's story is different:

Roger loved to sleep cuddled up with Nancy. A favorite pleasure while they were dating was to fall asleep with her in one arm, the other arm

> across her belly. Nancy tolerated this, because they slept together only twice a week. When they moved in together, the all-night cuddle didn't work for her. After several weeks, she felt irritable as bedtime approached. When she told Roger that cuddling all night really didn't work for her, he was deeply disappointed. In telling their stories to each other, they discovered unpleasant pieces of their childhoods that were contributing to their present problem
>
> Nancy's father, Jack, was a salesman who began traveling frequently when she began her pre-adolescent years. Nancy's mother, Lily, with whom she had a difficult relationship, became very lonely when Jack was away. Lily made Nancy sleep with her, and to her daughter's annoyance, held her tightly all through the night. When Nancy objected, Lily told her that she was selfish and unaffectionate. Now, Nancy was feeling the same bristly reaction when Roger wanted to sleep in a cuddling position all night.
>
> Roger's parents, Rose and Sol, were aloof and distant. From the age of three, they had stopped tucking him in bed, insisting that he "be a little man" and put himself to bed. While he soon learned to act brave in order not to incur his parents' disapproval, going to bed became a lonely time for Roger. His stuffed bear, Juno, which he held tightly during the night, became a source of deep comfort to him. When Nancy needed to sleep not touching, his old feelings of bedtime loneliness came back to him.

In telling their stories to each other, Nancy and Roger deepened their understanding of each other and of their problem. As well as giving ourselves the time we need to explore all the aspects of a problem, it is important to be honest in telling our stories to one another. We should not hide the truth. One responsible way to do this is to use words that claim our own responsibility for our own feelings. Instead of, "You hurt me very badly when you did that," a way in which we more honestly claim our own responsibility is to say, "I felt hurt when you said/did that. I'm wondering what was going on with you."

Give Yourself Time

Alphas often have a great sense of urgency to get the matter resolved *immediately* and the discussion closed out right now. We want to be done with it as quickly as possible. Inside, and unfortunately sometimes outside, we are saying some version of "For the love of God! Do I really have to endure yet another two-hour 'warm and fuzzy' time-waster episode?! Can't we just get this fucking hand-wringing done and over *efficiently?"* This sense of urgency may actually be a reliable sign that we still have at least a couple of toes in Powerland.

The time scale in Loveland is much more leisurely than the time scale in Powerland. When people buy flowers and other "sorry" gifts for their partners, it is sometimes an attempt to sidestep the need to talk through everything at the seemingly glacial pace that actually may be required to truly resolve and reconnect.

Take it slow. Initially, allow all of your partner's digressions, explanations, and excuses to stand; allow the exploration to deepen. Do not confront; instead, lead the discussion to a mutual exploration of the nature, background, priorities, emotions, and specific behaviors of each participant. Tolerate complexity, tolerate not yet having a full understanding of the problem, and tolerate (but do not give in to) your desire to "fix it quick". Connected Curiosity will help.

Connected Curiosity

We practice Connected Curiosity when we look our partner in the eyes with openness and ask *them* more questions about *their* experience (thoughts, feelings, perceptions) of the current issue. This is really hard to do when some Powerland part of our committee wants to either turn and leave them, kill them, hurt them, or shut them up, and then lecture them about why they are wrong and we are right. That committee member can be *screaming* at us inside. This is the time for our inner coach to remind that screaming Powerland team member that they have no place in this discussion. It is the time for the inner coach to send that Powerland member outside the door, where they belong, guarding the house. The coach can say, "It's Duct Tape time in Loveland tonight."

About Duct Tape

Applying duct tape is our metaphor for keeping our mouth shut when we want to scream, put our partner off rudely, or say or do something we will regret. Literally, we act as if we have duct tape over our mouth when we wish we had poison darts instead. Our image of stopping our negative emotions from translating into angry words and actions is Duct Tape. The picture we have is carrying a big roll of Duct Tape so you can tape your lips and you can also tape yourself to the chair, so that you can't get up from your chair and do bad things.

Directions for applying Duct Tape are as follows:

1. Remember that you are smart.
2. Remember that you have lots of inhibitory fibers that can damp down your emotions, *if you commit to the principle of not acting or speaking badly just because you feel badly* in the moment. You *can* stop yourself.
3. Be quiet. Imagine that you have Duct Tape across your mouth.
4. Imagine that you have Duct Tape strapping you to your chair.
5. Listen, intently.
6. Deep breathing during the above steps helps, a lot.

What's More Important? Being Right, or Being Married?

We can be right, or we can be partnered. We can either hammer our partner with our truth, or we can invest ourselves in getting both truths on the table. We must listen to our partner with the same sort of fascination with which we listened when we first fell in love. Does this mean we have to be our partner's therapist? Of course not.

When we first fell in love, we spent countless hours gazing into our partner's eyes and asking them all sorts of questions. While it is more difficult to begin doing this when we are standing on the shores of Powerland, hoping to get our boat back to Loveland, we can use our power in the service of love to begin the hard work of really listening to and getting to know our partner, not only when they are charming, but when they are damned difficult. Here is how Nancy and Roger's story continued.

> As Nancy told Roger about her mother's clinginess when her father traveled, Roger asked Nancy more questions about her experience. Nancy began to trust Roger's desire to really know her. She shared with him that in addition to some of the irritability that was a prior response from being forced to sleep with her mother, she had other feelings around Roger's nighttime touching. She loved Roger, she felt attentive to his needs. When his touch in the night awakened her, she became attuned with him in ways that made it difficult to sleep. Even before Roger told her about his teddy bear, Nancy related that she felt like a teddy bear. Her curiosity about Roger's bedtime ritual sparked Roger's memories of his lonely childhood bedtime. Each partner now understood themselves and the other better.

Connected Curiosity helps each of you come to a mutual understanding of the problem. Do not problem-solve until a mutually agreed upon understanding of the disconnect can be confirmed by multiple feedback loops.

Feedback Loops

Feedback Loops are exercises we do to make sure that we understand our partner's perspective and they understand ours. Feedback loops occur when each person retells their partner's tale in a way that does not shame, frighten, or enrage the other; rather, it lets them know that we understand (or not) the problem from their perspective. If we don't understand it, then we keep participating in the feedback loops until we do. In participating in a feedback loop, start the loop by saying something like, "Okay, let's see if I understand the crisis the way you do."

1. Then, as non-judgmentally as possible, recount the facts as you understand them.
2. If your partner has a different recounting of the facts, incorporate those

if you agree, or if you disagree, matter-of-factly note the difference.

3. Describe the results, again non-judgmentally, and your emotional responses as well as your understanding of your partner's emotional responses.
4. Describe, as you understand it, each partner's contributions to the crisis.
5. Listen carefully as your partner responds. Don't try to convince your partner that your point of view is correct. The point of the discussion is to learn together, not to win an argument.
6. If your partner becomes defensive, stay curious and open. Do not respond by becoming defensive yourself (Ludeman and Erlandson, p. 168).

Multiple feedback loops may be necessary until you both agree on the facts leading up to the crisis, each partner's emotional response to the crisis, and each partner's contribution to the crisis. If you can not agree on the facts leading up to the crisis, feedback loops should be engaged in until you both agree on the facts upon which you still disagree. You can disagree on the facts and most often, still move forward if you agree that you disagree about them.

Marty and Leslie's feedback loops and Marty's ability to tell the story from Leslie's perspective went like this:

> Subsequent to endless unpacking, Marty finally was able to tell Leslie's story from her perspective.
>
> "Oh," said Marty. "You mean any activity I initiate at any level, of any type, that increases the energy between us after 9 P.M. is pestiferously unwelcome to you. And no matter how I fix it, alter it, modify it, sweeten it up, whatever, it's still going to be unwelcome. The only things that are welcome are my winding down with you at that time or my absolute absence. Have I got it now?"
>
> Leslie smiled sweetly and said, "You've got it."
>
> And Leslie said, "What I understand is that you would like a lively companion for activities after 9:00 P.M. on those nights that we both agree we will be up after that hour. Have I got it?
>
> "You've got it," says Marty.

Telling the Story from Your Partner's Perspective

The goal of feedback loops is to be able to tell the story from our partner's perspective. We know our own perspective well. Until we can tell the story from our partner's point of view and claim our own responsibility, we are not doing our part to move our relationship back to Loveland. So, as we tell our stories in the unpacking part of the process, it is as important that we listen closely as it is that we speak honestly.

As we share our stories, it is only human, and certainly alpha, to be much more interested in talking and being heard than in listening to the other. It is easy to "want to make our point," to "be right." While our partner is speaking of their experience, their fears, their concerns, their anger, we find ourselves thinking about how we will respond instead of deeply listening. For people who claim that they want to live in Loveland, in a loving, trusting, cooperative, collegial place, it is important that they are able to explain a relationship problem from their partner's perspective as well as their own.

Here is how Pat and her sister Mary told the story from each others' perspective after unpacking the story of their restaurant fight:

> Pat: Let's see. We thought we were done processing the problem that arose earlier this afternoon, so we both agreed to have a glass of wine on our last dinner in this town. You thought you were making an innocuous remark to me about me. I thought we were going to laugh and celebrate working through our problem, so I made a remark back. One thing led to another, so by the time the delicious dinner that you had anticipated all afternoon arrived, an argument was heating up. You felt angry that the dinner was being spoiled by our arguing, put a "Halt!" hand signal up to me, then abruptly got up, left the table, and went out on the porch to cool off. You did this because you were afraid you were going to say something you would regret.
>
> I felt inflamed that you had started the conversation and then when I wanted to respond, you were telling me to halt. When you left to go to the porch, I felt really abandoned. I felt shame, and then rage about that. I didn't know how long you were planning to be on the porch, the dinner was now ruined for me, so I paid the bill and left. Even as I was doing it, I knew I shouldn't. Now I feel ashamed and really sorry about that.
>
> Mary: And when you paid for the dinner and left, by the time I returned to the table, my dinner had been cleared! Not only was I angry about missing our anticipated dinner, I felt abandoned. We had walked through a shady neighborhood on the way to the restaurant. We packed our large flashlight in my big purse before leaving and had

agreed to watch each others' backs. I felt very worried about your walking home alone, and betrayed that you weren't worried about me, that you had broken your promise to watch my back. You, however, had thought about those things, counted on your karate skills to keep you safe, knew that I had the flashlight and concluded that I would be all right.

You had also told yourself that if anyone looked really dangerous, you would turn around and find me. The people you saw along the way were homeless people who appeared harmless. Not knowing this, I felt enraged at being abandoned by you. When I reached the boat, I needed to know that you had gotten back safely. I was so mad I was afraid I would say something really terrible, and I didn't want to offend my best friend and sister. Also, I didn't want you more offended at me, so I packed my bag and left the boat.

Pat: And I felt really angry and abandoned that you were leaving without telling me where you were going, and then really worried for your safety.

Mary: I can certainly understand that.

Pat and Mary apologized to each other for their egregious behavior. They negotiated that if either needed a cool-off time out, they would state it in a neutral way, and that the other would respect that. And they agreed on no more abrupt leave-takings on either end, no matter what. They also agreed that if they got into a heated discussion at a restaurant, they would put it on the shelf when the food arrived, and that they would resume the conversation at a mutually agreed-upon time.

Talking to Others About Your Problem

Learning to tell the story from your partner's perspective is not only important when you are telling the story with your partner, it is also important when you are seeking help from others for yourself and for the relationship. At times we all turn to our friends for support and sometimes for help with a difficult problem in our marriage.

A Circle of Friends and Community

Terrence Real (2007) encourages keeping relationship practice growing and strong by connecting with others who are on a similar journey.

> When I'm upset or confused, I'm blessed with a number of people I can call who will support me and who will also be very frank about what they see. We all need that. Ideally, we can turn to a few trusted individuals and also a group setting or two (Real, 2007, p.272).

Pat loves the Episcopal wedding ceremony. When the couple says their marriage vows, the priest then turns to the congregation and asks them if they are willing to support this couple in their marriage journey. The congregation responds with an "I do."

We can choose our committee of caring friends, but if we come to that friend telling detailed gruesome stories about our partner, we are one big part of the problem. A true friend will want to support us *and* the relationship. The Loveland task for the friend is to help us prepare to reconnect with our partner when we have disconnected. The friend can support the reconnection by helping us unpack our own interests, hurts, and sensitivities. A friend helps us clarify and organize so that we are ready to go to the next stage of negotiation with our partner. What we do *not* want to do when we turn to our friends is to use the precious time that we have with them figuring out how to manipulate, intimidate, or trick our partner into complying with our wishes.

When someone comes to Marty's office telling gruesome stories about their partner, he asks them what their telling the story in this way has to do with Loveland. "How will my hating and despising your partner aid you in reconnecting with your partner?" Marty asks them to explain the situation with details only to the degree necessary to understand the situation.

If, when you speak to a friend or counselor, you tell the story in a dramatic way with much detail about your loathsome partner who ought to be ashamed of who they are and of doing what they are doing, the relationship is in trouble. What is coming out of your mouth is persecution from the victim stance of the drama triangle.

Now, back to how to process lovingly during a crisis. Once you understand the story from your partner's perspective as well as your own, and have some agreement about the events leading up to the disconnect, you are ready to address the problem. For starters, an apology is often appropriate.

Apologies

If we have caused harm through ignorance or neglect, we need to hear details about the harm that we have caused. Then we can figure out what was or was not going on in our head that we would have been so stupid, or unthinking, or unknowing. Then it becomes a solvable problem or a situation to be mutually managed. Once we understand more about the other person, we are never going to be ignorant in the same way again. We may forget for a moment, there will be a learning curve until we become reliable, but we will never be ignorant in the same way again.

When we discover that we have failed ourselves and said the unspeakable, there will be an Oh, Shit! moment with its attendant shame. We must be careful not to jump to Powerland from our shame place. If we do, we might find ourselves blaming our partner for their bad feelings in response to our behavior. Instead, say, "I forgot! I'm never supposed to say *that!*" Then we apologize, because even though we didn't mean to, we failed to live up to a commitment we made not to do that. Ignorance is not a defense. The first time that we hurt our partner out of ignorance, it is a learning experience; the second time and every time after that (which should get fewer and fewer) is an opportunity to apologize. The only other choice is to deepen our stupidity. If we have unintentionally done harm, we ask ourselves, in our partner's presence, "What was I thinking?" and move towards understanding what we did from our partner's point of view.

When a mutually agreed-upon understanding of the disconnect is confirmed and appropriate apologies made, we are now ready to make a request and listen to our partner's request for solutions. Solutions are best arrived at through knowing our own priorities as well as those of our partner, then negotiating based on our awareness of those priorities.

Learning to Negotiate

There are no communication problems with literate adults. There are only communication efforts that should not have been started in the first place. Why not? Because they are "Power Over" communications. They are communications that say, "If I just badger you enough, or say it enough, you will do what I want; you'll come around." Lots of luck with this. What will come around is something you don't want, and not what you are working for, if you really want to get back to Loveland.

The term "communication problems" is usually a disguised code for power plays by one or both parties. In an alpha/beta pairing, saying, "Look, we're having communication problems" can usually be translated as, "Look, I'm not getting my way." When a beta is claiming communication problems, it is usually from a drama triangle victim position. The victim will often engage in behaviors such as whining, begging, avoidance, collapsing, and getting sick, and is therefore unavailable.

If you are not trained in negotiation, you may have to go get a "How To" book on the subject (the stores are full of them). The best such book that we know is *Getting to Yes* by Roger Fisher, William Ury, and Bruce Patton (1991). The basic thesis of this book is that people negotiate from and for their interests, so that through the process of negotiation, both parties can have their interests satisfied to some significant degree. This is a model that stands in stark contrast to one partner getting everything they want through intimidation, competition and/or trickery. Learning negotiation skills can help you stand in your own shoes, explain your own boundaries, explain your side of the problem in a non-hurtful way, listen to and understand the other's point of view, and be respectful of their boundaries. This book helps the reader get clear about their priority interest, so that secondary interests might be sacrificed in service to the relationship.

> When Marty and Leslie negotiated their problem related to different needs around bedtime, Marty's primary interest was having evenings full of fun and joviality, preferably with Leslie. Leslie's priority was to sleep. Those two things could not be done in the same space: something had to change. One of Marty's secondary interests, spontaneity, had to become just that, secondary.
>
> We will tell you more about how Marty and Leslie arrived at a management plan for their problem in Chapter Twelve. For now, suffice it to say that as part of their management plan, arrived at through eighteen months of storytelling, trial and error and negotiation, Marty still has fun in the evenings, but mostly by himself. Two nights a week, he has the pleasure of Leslie's company for a date night. If they are to be out late, they must carefully plan together for her to nap during the day prior to the event. If he had to be alone *every* night of the week, that would be too much of a sacrifice. If Leslie could not get enough sleep every night of the week, that would be too much to ask of her. Each party's primary interest was satisfied. Since Marty identified spontaneity as a secondary need, he was able to sacrifice that, so that evenings together could be carefully planned, as they had to be in order for Leslie to join him. Conversely, Marty goes to bed early any time he wants, as long as he winds down before hand, comes to bed in a timely fashion, and saves his exuberantly funny stories for the morning.

Defining the Type of Problem

Some problems and some solutions are obvious. If you were ignorant, you claim it. If you were neglectful, you claim it. If you were unintentionally hurtful, you apologize. Often, however, problems are not obvious. In the next chapters we present our taxonomy of problems that organizes the seemingly endless myriad of simple and complex problems couples encounter. We have grouped all problems, simple and complex, into four categories. We define them, and we offer effective management techniques for each of them.

CHAPTER TEN

DISAPPOINTMENTS

There are basically only four kinds of problems in any significant relationship that can put us in crisis and, if we allow it, quickly whisk us out of Loveland and into Powerland. In the following three chapters we are going to describe these problems and provide tools for addressing them.

A word of caution: Many of the examples used in the following chapters are those of real couples confronting real problems and arriving at real solutions that allow them to live in Loveland. However, the stories of their processes have been condensed. While the stories and solutions may seem simple, sometimes it can take weeks or even months of revisiting a problem, sharing stories and experiences, and devising and trying solutions, before workable solutions are achieved.

Remember, the basic tenet that must be present in order to live in Loveland is *absence of malice*. That means that any willingness to hurt our partner, which is business-as-usual behavior in Powerland, must be absent in our relationship. In the absence of malice, there are only four types of problems that can occur. Before you become too reassured and think that now things will be simple, we must tell you that if you are an alpha male or female, addressing these problems will be one of the hardest things you will ever do in your life. Clip your nails, because you are going to want to hang on hard to the cliffs of Powerland. If you clip your nails, the scratches on the cliffs won't be as deep, and your fingernails will be less raw when you let go and begin your journey to Loveland. Letting go will feel like surrender. Don't panic! In the absence of malice, surrender is a form of relaxation. You won't die. We promise. It will only feel like it initially.

In the absence of malice, these are the only four causes of emotional pain in a relationship: 1. Disappointments 2. Interruptions 3. Inconveniences 4. Irreconcilable Differences. These can occur separately, or sometimes one event will be two or three, or even all four wrapped in one!

The First Cause of Emotional Pain is Disappointment

Disappointments happen when our expectations are not met. We fall in love. Not only are we aware of many wonderful attributes of our new love, we also *imagine* many attributes that may not be there. We may imagine that our partner will always want to make love when we do, or will want the same amount of space and closeness that we do, or will want to join us in our hobbies, or will have similar eating or sleeping habits.

Remember, most of the good news is already visible early (by the first three to four months) in a relationship. The surprises increasingly tend to be negative surprises. That equals disappointments. No one can act on their best behavior forever, and no one is going to have exactly all the attributes for which we would wish and dream.

Disappointment as a Function of Expectations

What is crucial to understand about a disappointment is that it is always a solvable problem because it is a function of our own expectations. There cannot be a disappointment unless you have an expectation in the first place. You cannot be disappointed without an expectation, and you are in charge of your expectations.

The good news is that the person who is disappointed is always in control of the situation, because they arbitrarily selected their expectations. They can't ever proclaim that the reason they are unhappy is solely some external event or characteristic of the partner. In order to feel unhappy, they had to have had an expectation in advance. No one is entitled to have every expectation they want fulfilled, nor is anyone else required to meet someone's expectations at all times. Expectations are always negotiable.

The only expectation that is not negotiable is that each partner in the relationship gets to expect NOT to be treated maliciously. Malice and harm are non-negotiable. In the absence of malice, ALL expectations are negotiable, either within one's self or between two partners. Disappointments, unfulfilled expectations, are a crisis in a relationship, but always a negotiable crisis.

Commonly Experienced Disappointments

There are many arenas in a relationship around which disappointments can occur. Here is a checklist of some of those disappointments, as well as room to write in your own.

1. Different bedtimes and bedtime rituals. Marty likes to stay up late; Leslie needs to go to bed early.
2. Different needs around amount of time to be together and separate. Upon his retirement, Austin expected that his wife, Mary, would drop her separate hobbies and golf with him on a daily basis.
3. Different food habits. June loves meals cooked with lots of vegetables. George, a meat and potatoes man, hates vegetables.
4. Different hobbies. Dan loves to sail. His wife, Pat, prefers to garden in her spare time.
5. Differing needs for physical affection. Charles grew up in a family who taught him that physical shows of affection, such as hugging and kissing, should be reserved for the home. His wife, Clarice, grew up in an Italian family, where public demonstrations of affection were common.
6. Different needs around sex. When Ross is anxious, sex helps him relax. Talking doesn't. Jill needs to relax by talking and emotionally connecting before she can have sex.
7. Incompatible styles of negotiation. Sue demands the last word. Will avoids initiating any negotiation. Therefore, Sue gets to start *and* finish every negotiation.
8. Different styles and expectations about humor. Male locker room humor is almost universally not funny to women, especially if applied to them. A wet towel to the ass is not good foreplay.
9. Different needs around relationships with children, in-laws, friends, business partners, pets. Jan deeply needs regular time with women friends; her husband Bob wishes Jan would spend all her socializing time with him.
10. Different customs regarding social obligations. Jeff, an attorney, belongs to the country club and is active in his alumni association, because he meets potential clients there. His wife Delores is introverted and detests these gatherings.
11. Different needs and habits around money. Joe grew up in a thrifty New England family with a value of doing most work self-sufficiently. Sue grew up in a wealthy Southern family where it was commonplace to

hire many tasks done.

12. Different expectations and attitudes regarding politics. One liberal spouse, one conservative spouse.
13. Different needs and expectations in religion and religious orientation. Jack grew up in an atheist family; his wife Mary is a devout Roman Catholic.
14. Different beliefs about appropriate manners in public places. Sean is embarrassed when his demonstrative Italian wife Lola either kisses him or yells at him in public.

Reader, can you think of others? Any nit we haven't picked? List disappointments that you encounter in your relationship:

About Grieving

Disappointments happen in significant relationships. When they are big ones, it is important that we grieve them; there is nothing wrong with this. Grieving means allowing ourselves to feel sad, and internally angry, that we are not going to get what we expected. We need to give ourselves time to experience those feelings. We may need ten minutes, or several days, or sometimes more. It is okay to tell your partner that you are having feelings around your disappointment. It is not okay to blame your partner for your bad feelings. When you do that, you are being both victim and persecutor on the drama triangle, while secretly hoping that your partner will rescue you by agreeing never to disappoint you in that way again. Remember, you are the author of your expectations, which are the source of your disappointment and consequent grief. Your partner's disappointing performance is a *secondary* issue, and ultimately negotiable when you have dealt with your feelings enough to negotiate without malice. The *primary* issue is living happily in Loveland with your partner.

Terrence Real (2000), in his book *How Can I Get Through to You?* talks about the griefs and losses we experience in relationships:

> There are things you get in a real relationship, and things you do not get. The character of the union is determined by how the two partners manage both aspects of love—the getting and the not getting. Moving into acceptance means moving into grief, without being a victim. You own your choice. "I am getting enough in this relationship," you say, "to make it worth my while to mourn the rest." And mourn we do. Real love is not for the faint of heart. What we miss in our relationships we truly miss. The pain of it does not, and need not, go away. It is like dealing with any loss (p. 224).

Sometimes we may not have enough beef to have an all-beef burger; sometimes we need to add some soy extender. But it is still a nourishing and good-tasting meal.

DEALING WITH DISAPPOINTMENT

1. Be honest with yourself and your partner about your disappointed expectation.
2. Grieve your unmet expectation.
3. You may need to voice your disappointment to your partner in a way that also respects their inability or unwillingness to meet your expectations.
4. Together, explore a different expectation that, in light of what you have learned about your partner, you can arbitrarily choose in the same way that you chose your initial expectation. This expectation can now be more in line with the reality of who your partner really is, and therefore less susceptible to disappointment. Make sure it is one you believe you

and your partner can live with.

5. Explore with your partner whether the new expectation is one that is reasonable and achievable for them.
6. Practice, practice, practice.
7. Big differences in expectations and performance will require review, updates, and renegotiations. Even successfully negotiated solutions will require the same. This is because life cycles change and present us with new situations as previously unaddressed nuances and subtleties in our differences will emerge.
8. When your expectations are fine-tuned and your partner's performances are fine-tuned and flowing, celebrate!

Pat's Story: Bill was 65 and Pat was 45 when they married. Bill was an attorney, Pat was a therapist, and each was active in their respective professional organizations. Bill's previous two wives had accompanied him to four professional conferences that he attended yearly. The second wife easily accompanied him because she worked in the same field. Often, Pat was unable to accompany Bill to his conferences; two of them usually conflicted with the timing of her own professional meetings. Most of the other attorneys' wives did not work and had less busy schedules. Additionally, the activities planned for the wives were frequently ones Pat did not enjoy, such as shopping trips and manicures.

Bill was initially disappointed. While he was quite capable of socializing at the dinners and dances when he was alone, he was proud of his beautiful, vibrant wife and he wanted Pat to be there, like the wives of the other members.

Bill shared his disappointment with Pat. She shared her discomfort with the activities for the wives, her need to do something different with her time, and the conflict she had with her need to attend her own professional conferences. They listened to one another with increasing understanding. Bill gave up his expectation that Pat would accompany him to every conference and that she would accompany him for the full time of each conference. Pat agreed to go with Bill when he was making an important presentation, receiving an award at his conferences, or sometimes for the weekend days in fun locations, when it did not conflict with her conferences. On these occasions, she was able to go for one or two days, have fun supporting Bill, and then leave without compromising time from her meetings or other parts of her life. Bill, who was a fantastic dancer, became a hit with other wives whose husbands did not enjoy dancing. When Pat attended the conferences, she enjoyed their compliments to him, his joy in their compliments, and their exclamations that she was a very lucky woman. They felt satisfied that they had worked this out well.

CHAPTER ELEVEN

INTERRUPTIONS

Interruptions are different from disappointments. In a disappointment, you are expecting something from someone else in your web of love, and that's not what happens. That's not what they deliver.

In an interruption, you are not expecting anything from anyone. You are happily doing what you are doing, and your significant other or someone else in your web of love comes and stops you. Or, you are doing something together and someone or something else interrupts the two of you in your togetherness. The interruption may happen lovingly. No matter; still a bummer. Even if you are lovingly interrupted, you are being interrupted from something you are happily doing.

You are going along happily with yourself, or with others, and you aren't even thinking about an interruption. Your partner or someone else wasn't even on your screen. Someone has to unexpectedly insert themselves into your experience, onto the computer screen of your life, in order for an interruption to happen.

If the interruption occurs with your partner (if for example, you are cuddling on the sofa, you are hoping you will make love, and your partner falls asleep) you have not only an interruption in the sense that they have stopped the good stuff that was happening. You also had the *expectation* that they were going to continue to cooperate in the deliverance of the good stuff that was happening, so now you have an interruption *and* a disappointment. *Coitus Interruptus!*

An alpha response to an interruption is to blame the other for interrupting and to chastise them in such a way that they will never do it again. Here are some examples. You may know them well:

> "Can't you see I'm busy?!"
>
> "What's the matter with you? I'm watching the ballgame!"
>
> "You're spoiling my fun!"
>
> "How dare you call! Me and the guys were just getting our poker game going."
>
> "There's always some reason you fall asleep when I want to make love! You hate sex!"

Interruptions from Others

When a couple is happily enjoying each others' company, interruptions are unwelcome. Even if the interruption comes from a well-intended or loving place, it is experienced as annoying, or worse.

> Ken and Maria enjoy their morning coffee ritual. They live in a small town; their favorite spot is the corner Starbucks. There they often read a poem or morning meditation together and discuss it over coffee before planning their day. One day Stan, a friend Ken had not seen for some time, passed by, noticed Ken, jovially approached their table and asked if he might join them. Stan shared that he had recently moved into the neighborhood and that the Starbucks was on his morning walk route. While Ken was glad to reconnect with his old friend, he and Maria both felt irritated with the interruption of their morning ritual.
>
> When this happened several more times, they devised a plan. Ken arranged a meeting at the Starbucks with Stan. He told him of his and Maria's morning ritual and that while he would like to spend some time with him, he and Maria would like to protect their morning ritual. He invited Stan for a guy's game of racquetball, followed by dinner with him and Maria.

Maria and Ken felt pleased with how they had handled Stan's interruption. They negotiated ways in which they would handle future interruptions. They had some differences about this (a disappointment). Maria preferred informing the interrupting party in the moment. Ken grew up in the South, where you just don't do that. He preferred speaking to the person later, as he had with Stan, or making an excuse to leave and changing locations. After successful negotiation, they agreed that if the interrupting party were an acquaintance of Maria's, she would address the issue directly with them at the time of interruption. If the interrupting acquaintance were one of Ken's, he would announce that they were just leaving, and/or speak with them later.

Interruptions by Your Partner

An interruption can happen when you are doing something alone or with someone else and your partner interrupts, lovingly or otherwise.

Sara treasured her time with her best friend Beth, who had dropped by for a visit shortly after Sara and Mark had moved in together. Mark was at work and not expected home until the end of the day. Sara had just brewed a pot of tea, served herself and Beth, and settled down in her favorite easy chair across from Beth for a long "girl talk." Fifteen minutes later, Mark burst through the door. "Hi, Honey! I'm home! I got the afternoon off work and rushed home. Thought we might clean that closet like we had talked about."

Sara was angry. She had an expectation that Mark would have called her if he were coming home early. She was experiencing a disappointed expectation as well as an interruption. What Sara *didn't* say was, "I'm not a box of dried, instant Sara that you can reconstitute at a moment's notice!" Whew! She asked Beth to excuse her and Mark for a moment. She and Mark went into the kitchen. Sara shared her desire to spend time alone with Beth. Mark was flexible, remembered a film that he wanted to see and decided that this afternoon would be a good time to see it. They made an appointment for after dinner to discuss their different expectations about calling home before appearing unexpectedly and how they might handle future similar interruptions.

Interruptions by Mood and/or Behavior

An interruption can happen when you are doing something lovingly with your partner and a mood or behavior on their part interrupts your good feelings. There may be different understandings between you and your partner about what you are doing, or are going to do, with your time. Again, you have not only an interruption in the sense that they have stopped the good stuff that was happening, but you had the *expectation* that they were going to continue to cooperate in the deliverance of the good stuff. You have an interruption *and* a disappointment.

> Chad and Margaret had spent the evening cuddled on the sofa, engaged in one of their favorite activities, watching movies. Chad had rented two movies from the video store. After pizza, he had begun the first movie, saving the second, which he was really anticipating, for "best last." At 9:00 p.m. when the first movie ended, Margaret yawned and announced that she was going to bed; she was more than usually tired from her workday.
>
> Chad couldn't believe it! They had known each other for a year, and they had always watched two movies on their "movie nights!" Margaret's fatigue was an interruption of their good time. It was also a disappointed expectation for Chad.

Every engagement or disengagement has the possibility of being experienced as an interrupt by either party. If one partner has difficulty with disengagement and experiences disengagement as a big interruption of joy, partners may need to carefully plan etiquette for disengagement. A disengagement does not have to be a disconnect, but it can turn into one if one partner has difficulty with disengagement and a plan is not made for addressing it.

> Gina was a professional woman whose work sometimes took her away from home. In addition, she had many outside interests that she greatly valued. Peter was a homebody. He worked out of an office at home and he pursued woodworking hobbies in a home workshop. His greatest joy in life was when he and Gina were home together. While he understood Gina's need to be away, he would often become sulky and hurt on mornings she was about to leave. As he withdrew, their leave-takings also turned into disconnects. They both hated parting in this way. With connected curiosity, Gina asked Peter what would make her leaving less painful for him. After some thought, Peter decided that snuggle time in the morning would help, as well as some reminders of her presence while she was gone. Gina was willing to awaken half an hour earlier for snuggle times. She was also able to creatively think of ways she could remind Peter of her presence while she was gone. She left notes and cards, reminders of her love, in places where Peter would find them as he went about his day. Peter was also willing to take responsibility for his hurt and loneliness. He found a beautiful rock that Gina had given him early in their dating. He kept the rock in his pocket as a reminder of Gina's solid love for him while she was away.

Reengagement after a time apart can also be experienced as an interruption. We get accustomed to not having to negotiate when differences arise, because there are none when we are alone. We get to have it all our own way! We may like quiet time, as in Joyce and Stephen's story, below.

> Stephen loved Joyce. He loved sharing his life with her, and he also treasured his time alone at home while Joyce was on business trips. Each had lived alone for some years before they met and moved in together in their fifties. Each had been set in their ways before moving in together. Stephen loved to sleep in very cool air; Joyce liked the bedroom warm and cozy. Each night before bedtime, they would assess the temperature and agree on some compromise.
>
> One night, Joyce arrived home just about bedtime. After a hello hug, she unthinkingly marched to the thermostat and turned it up. After all, she had been doing that the whole two weeks while she was away! Stephen had also enjoyed not having to negotiate about the night time temperature. They were both tired. A fight ensued.
>
> One of them had the good sense, using their power in the service of love, to stop bickering over the temperature and ask the other what this really might be about. This gave the other a chance to pause and reflect upon the interruption of reentry. "When I'm by myself, I can just set the thermostat any damn way I want! No conversation necessary!" The other laughed and admitted to feeling that also. As they talked, they made a plan. Whenever possible, Joyce would arrange her travel schedule to be home by dinnertime. They would set that time aside for a special dinner and would each talk about their time apart, giving them time to come back into the space of togetherness, to leave the space of apartness.

Changes, positive and negative ones, can be interruptions. It is important to notice this, and to negotiate a plan, as Stephen and Joyce did, to address these. Notice your disconnects. Address them. After a number of these negotiations around different interruptions, it becomes possible to see if there is an underlying problem. If there is, and it is found, it provides for deeper and more long-lasting solutions.

> Gina had a desire for reassurance through direct contact with her partner, Bob. She frequently would approach Bob wanting a hug and an "I love you." Bob, however, was perfectly happy without direct contact, simply knowing Gina was around, doing her own thing. He experienced Gina's advances for physical contact and words of endearment as an interruption when he was absorbed in whatever he was doing. They resolved their difference by negotiating check-in rituals so that when

they were in the same space, every two hours each would take a "time out" to make contact with the other. Gina got her needed physical and verbal contact. Bob could plan his time, knowing that he would not be interrupted over the course of two hours. Remember, the point is continuous connection, even while apart. The strategy here, as with disappointments, is to treat the interruptions as solvable problems that can be worked out through careful and caring negotiations to prevent repetition.

Dealing with Interruptions

When an interruption happens for the first time, it can result in the Oh Shit!" whoosh to Powerland. The first interruption has already happened; we can't fix that one. *But interruptions are negotiable and solvable problems* when mutually agreeable rules about how and when we engage and disengage are set up so that we feel good about the rules and about each other.

Here is what we can do:

1. After each partner has told their story, identify the disconnect as an interruption. If it is also a disappointment, identify that also.
2. Look at the patterns involved, and the ways in which the disconnect has occurred. If your partner has interrupted, remember your commitment to absence of malice. Looking at the ways in which the disconnect has occurred does not mean considering your partner to be a thoughtless, insensitive person. Absence of malice means assuming the best of your partner; that however they interrupted, it was done in innocence or ignorance. Ignorance does not imply something bad. Ignorance simply means that your partner was not in possession of information that they now have.
3. Negotiate using the following questions:
   a. How do we interrupt each other in a way that works for each of us?
   b. How do we engage each other in a way that works for each of us?
   c. How do we make the transition from engagement to disengagement; from disengagement to engagement?
   d. How do we make both the engagement and the disengagement as painless and/or non-disruptive as possible?
   e. When and how do we engage each other?

Exercise:

1. *Think about a time or times when you feel annoyed about your partner's interrupting you. Write this down.*

2. *If this reminds you of interruptions from your past, even in your childhood, write this down.*

3. *Write down your best guess about your partner's inner process in the interruption. That is, assuming the best intentions and highest level of innocence on your partner's part, what might be going on with them when they interrupt you?*

4. What information would you like for your partner to know about you in order to manage this interruption?

5. What information would you like from your partner about her or his process that would help you better understand their interrupting?

6. Engage your partner around these issues. See if you can come up with some mutually agreeable rules around this interruption.

Here is how Webb and Mia resolved a problem of interruption:

Webb is a college professor of classics and very introverted. Some of his favorite times are spent in his home office, reading the classics, contemplating their meaning and preparing his lectures. He enjoys the neat organized stacks of papers on his desk; his coffee cup also has its special place.

His partner, Mia, is an extroverted teacher of design at the same college. Her office is littered with fabric samples, paint samples, and drawings tacked around the walls. She welcomes interruptions, as an unexpected conversation may lead to a creative idea.

When they first moved in together, Webb was appalled when Mia opened the door to his office, sat down seductively on his desk, repositioned several of his stacks, began sipping his coffee, and enthusiastically told him about a breakthrough in her latest project. Before he knew what was happening, Webb exclaimed, "How dare you burst in here like this?!"

Upon addressing their disconnect and talking about their different work styles, they devised a solution. Webb installed a small light outside his office. When he wanted to work without interruption, he left the light on. If he was available for company, he turned off the light. He arranged the small table in his office corner with two chairs and two coffee mugs. He welcomed Mia's dropping in for a visit at the end of his lecture preparation.

CHAPTER TWELVE

INCOVENIENCES AND IRRECONCILABLE DIFFERENCES

Irreconcilable differences are strong preferences of each member of the couple that cannot be satisfied in the same place at the same time in some compatible way. Irreconcilable differences are incompatible strong preferences, not what the legal system defines as a convenient excuse for divorce. Marty and Leslie's bedtime preferences are an example of an irreconcilable difference. Incompatible strong preferences are manageable in a relationship.

An inconvenience is part of being human. Things break, they fail, people age. Things happen to one of the partners or the relationship itself. Inconveniences are the patina of life.

Inconveniences and irreconcilable differences are by definition not solvable problems. They are chronic unsolvable problems that at best can be managed well. Worse yet, they are generative of multitudes of little problems that, disappointingly, when solved, do not stop the inconvenience. An example of this might be creative and vicious stepchildren who continue to create little problems around holiday gatherings.

Each member of the couple always brings some part of themselves to a relationship that is so incompatible as to be highly inconvenient. It is not a part that will change; it won't go away. Irreconcilable differences are also inconveniences. Let's look at some of these.

While it may be unsettling and redundant, we must revisit the awareness that gender difference is a starting point of many inconveniences in relationships. Otherwise, we start thinking that our partner is "bad" or difficult. They are not. Men and women are trained differently and grow up in significantly different cultures. They work differently emotionally and cognitively. Men are more often trained to look out for themselves first, while women are trained to be aware of others' needs first and more often to be aware of all the needs of a group of people. Women's emotions are often more available to them. They also are better at articulating their emotions. Women think more systemically; men think in a more focused way. Women often enjoy and look forward to processing feelings and talking about problems; men dread it. Men often become impatient and want to "just fix it" rather than first talking about it at length (read *ad nauseum*).

Other factors that can be huge inconveniences in a relationship include individual differences brought from our families of origin, differing regions, public versus private schooling, and class disparities. Then there are major differences in our adult life experiences. For instance, one person has a chronic disease and is married to someone who has never been ill. Or someone from a very stable background may be partnered with a person who has been the victim of childhood abuse. There are diverse approaches to money, as well as different experiences with the use of alcohol and other substances.

It's not enough that our partner, in their makeup, brings the inconvenience of being different from us. To top it off, as life progresses we invariably encounter further inconveniences. We wear out, we get tired, we get old, things break, taxes have to be done. Pat's wonderful friends, Les and Jay, married at midlife, after knowing each other and loving each other for many years, truly knew they had met and were marrying the love of their life. The first two years of their marriage were blissful. Then Les was diagnosed with Parkinson's Disease. In addition to this being a grievous disappointment, it was a huge inconvenience.

Many additional items can be added to this list. We invite you to add your own irreconcilable differences to our list. Write them here.

Irreconcilable differences by definition won't go away. They can only (and must be) managed. They can be managed well, or they can be managed poorly, but there are no solutions that fix them once and for all. In managing these very inconvenient differences, it is important first to know that this is not just a disappointment, and that it is not just an interruption.

Because inconveniences and irreconcilable differences do not go away, managing them is more challenging than with disappointments or interruptions. With disappointments we can control our expectations. With interruptions we can problem-solve and set boundaries around engagement and disengagement. As an alpha, because even thinking about managing irreconcilable differences can be daunting, our first Powerland response is to think that if our partner would *just be like us*, the problem would go away. You know, why couldn't our partner:

> Be less emotional.
> Be more emotional.
> Go to bed at "a reasonable" time.
> Talk more.
> Talk less.
> Be neater.
> Not be so prissy.
> Be more organized.
> Not be so uptight; go more with the flow.
> Not be sick.
> Not age so soon.

The list is endless. And before we know it, if we continue to stay in Powerland around an inconvenience or an irreconcilable difference, we are using all kinds of Powerland ploys in a misguided and unworkable attempt to get our partner to change. We subtly guilt-trip them for being different, or for not feeling well, or for their habits. We propose "solutions" that involve their thinking or behaving or feeling more like we do. We overtly or covertly threaten to leave, or to withhold our love.

> Jonas hated it when his new wife, Marguerite, didn't want to have sex on his schedule. "You don't know what it means to be a couple!" was his Powerland ploy to attempt to make her more like him. "I have needs, you know, and if I can't get them met with you, I may have to go somewhere else," was his Powerland attempt to suggest abandonment through infidelity if Marguerite didn't "shape up."

Relationships, when pursued lovingly, can provide us with gentle healing of our narcissism. One aspect of narcissism is thinking that the world would be a better place if everyone were just more like us. If we want to live in Loveland, we have to come face to face with the fact that we as a couple have an inconvenience or an irreconcilable difference that must be managed. While inconveniences and irreconcilable differences are sometimes challenging to address, the rules are short:

1. Identify the disconnect.
2. Honor the commitment to absence of malice.
3. Unpack each partner's story.
4. Devise a management plan.

We told you we would finish Leslie and Marty's story. Here it is, their story about managing a huge irreconcilable difference around sleeping habits.

> For one and a half years, Marty and Leslie tried various solutions. Marty stayed up until he got sleepy and then went to bed hours later than Leslie had. When Marty came to bed after midnight, even with his best efforts to do so softly, Leslie would awaken and would face the morning without sufficient rest. Marty's snoring didn't help, thus further extending the disruption of Leslie's sleep.
>
> One night Leslie, hoping Marty would come to bed with her so that she wouldn't be awakened later and also wanting to enjoy his company as she snuggled in at her comfortable 9:30 hour, entreated him to come to bed with her. Marty had just gotten comfortable in his favorite chair, eagerly anticipating perusing a stack of journals. Her entreaty was an interruption. Furthermore, her need for this kind of bedtime was a big inconvenience to him; why couldn't she just be more like him? In the midst of an Oh Shit!! moment, he found himself in Powerland, with one of the mean tough guys on his committee speaking the following words out loud, "Why in the world would I want to come to bed with *you* right now?" (This is a barely concealed version of "Just get out of my way and leave me alone, bitch.")
>
> Leslie used her power, one aspect of which is her vulnerability, in the service of love. She burst into tears. Marty was immediately sorry for his words. They agreed to meet the next evening, early, to address this problem one more time. They sat down and "unpacked" the bedtime issue yet again. As they did so, each of them shared what their particular bedtime habits had meant to them growing up. They concluded that this particular issue was a big, irreconcilable difference. Neither was going to be able to conform to the other's bedtime habits. They cast about for a management plan. As they worked on ideas for managing this, they remembered that this had not been a problem before they moved in together. Their "date night" routine had worked very well. On date nights, if they were spending a cozy evening at home, Marty often accompanied Leslie to bed early. He didn't mind this, as he weekly had

the other five nights to stay up as late as he wanted, enjoying his late night pursuits. If they went out somewhere, or Leslie expected they would be up late talking or loving, she took a nap before Marty arrived. She also had five nights a week to go to bed early according to her usual habits.

They remembered the sitting room attached to their bedroom, which they had designated as a reading room. Their management strategy was to make this a bedroom for Leslie. The room was connected to their bedroom, so she and Marty could each rest with the assurance of each other's nearness. They added curtains to separate the two rooms, and a noise machine so that Leslie would not be disturbed by his arrival in the next room or by his snoring. Two nights a week, they designated as "date night." They managed these nights in the same way they had when they dated; sometimes Marty went to bed early and sometimes Leslie took a nap if they were going to be out late. Their management plan worked.

Everyone has different ways of managing inconveniences, so in order for you and your partner to have continuous connection in the absence of malice, you have to figure out how to manage your incompatible differences and inconveniences, including those that occur just by the process of living daily life: illnesses, relatives, friends, different values, changing values, or whatever. These differences and inconveniences must be managed in a way that keeps you continuously connected. Remember, an incompatible difference and/or an inconvenience won't go away. If you try to pretend that it will go away or try to use force or manipulation to get it to go away, you are not in Loveland, you are in Powerland and you are operating under malice.

The only thing that can be done is to come together and say, "Okay, we have a problem. We have a problem that really doesn't have a solution; let's see how we can manage it." Marty says about the bedtime difference between him and Leslie:

> We grew up so differently. We are together 24-7 because we both mostly work out of the home. How do we work this out? When we weren't living together, we had a solution; we dated and we lined ourselves up accordingly. Every date worked; we loved each other and we felt our connection. Then we were together 24-7 and nothing worked. It took one and a half years, and we did work it out, because we were committed to being without malice. It took us one and one half years to figure out that this wasn't a solvable problem; if only the other person would act normal, meet us halfway. There was really no halfway! Now, if she knows in advance that we're going to do something—go to a museum, dinner, a play, where we get home at midnight, she has a solution. She takes a nap in the afternoon and structures her day so she can do that. I don't have to do that, but for her, it has to be planned, and if she

doesn't get the nap, it doesn't work; we have to leave early. If we know in advance and something comes up and interferes with the nap plan, we know that we're going to have to plan to have a shorter evening. It happens very seldom, because we are, and I am, very careful of it. For example, I'm very careful to not be the reason her nap is interrupted. I want her there in good spirits; I don't want to have her leave me to come home early or be forced to come home early with her.

Every once in a while at 9:00 at night, I'll get a brilliant idea of something I want to discuss with her and she looks at me with bleary eyes and says, "It's 9:00."

"Yeah," I'll say. "But I had this great idea! It'll solve all the world's problems! Just give me 5 minutes!"

But it doesn't solve all the world's problems; it just creates problems. Her ears don't work after 9 P.M. Nothing's working! The first time, she'll say something like, "Can it wait till morning?"

I'll say, "I'm not going to *remember* it in the morning!"

We don't have this conversation any more because we've had it already. So, when that moment comes, I'll just look in her eyes and say, "Oh, OK; it'll come back." I'll write it down, whatever. At that point, for her, it doesn't much matter; the bed is calling.

From Leslie's perspective, she says, "I have learned that in the mornings, every morning, I have to be very careful not to say bouncy, happy, funny things, or ask much of Marty. He cannot do mornings, and when circumstances force him to "do" a morning (defined as the time before noon), he is not okay. So, I have to treat him as carefully in the morning as he has to treat me after 9:00 P.M."

Who would think that a problem as seemingly small as bedtime would be such a major one? When we fall in love and date, we believe that nothing like that could be a big problem. When we share the intimacies of day-to-day living together, in the words of a country singer, "It's the little things that piss me off."

While this story is condensed for our purposes here, Marty and Leslie's management package took one and a half years of talking, trying solutions and learning. They learned what didn't work from unworkable Powerland values and behaviors, such as Marty's rude statement ("Why would I want to come to bed with *you* right now?"). They also learned what didn't work from their trials of over-adaptive behaviors, such as Marty's attempts to go to bed at 9:00 P.M., or Leslie's efforts to compensate for inadequate sleep by taking naps, now not in order to stay up, but to catch up. They tried many things before they came up with an effective management plan. Yet it is obvious to the observer that they live in Loveland.

CHAPTER THIRTEEN

FINISHING

How do you know when you are done processing a crisis? Sometimes your body lets you know by a release of tense feelings. Many people have a tension spot that flares when they first disconnect. Typical spots (check for your own) are the head, face, throat, chest, solar plexus, belly and pelvis. Pat's is her face; when she experiences the shame associated with disconnection, she experiences something like a sheet of steel, simultaneously hot and cold flowing both up and down her face. Marty experiences tightness in his solar plexus, the power center of the body. When the reconnect occurs and is reconfirmed, the hot spot cools down.

One provisional way we can tell we are finished is that we feel connected again, loving and loved, trusting, safe and calm. There is often the feeling of accomplishment, perhaps accompanied by that good kind of fatigue when we have done something really hard; it took a lot of courage and effort, but together we got there.

You have a provisional understanding of the problem and how you got into it. You have determined whether it was a disappointed expectation, an interruption, or an inconvenience/irreconcilable difference, or some combination. You have a provisional solution if it is a disappointment or interruption, or you have a management package if it is a condition of inconvenience or irreconcilable difference.

The solution too is provisional; you don't know if it is going to work. You try it out, understanding that you may fail. You don't really know if you have understood the problem deeply enough or well enough until you try out your provisional solution. The presence or absence of failure is how you discover whether you really understood the problem fully and deeply or if there is more about the nature of the problem that you need to understand in order to better solve or manage the situation. That is why the process can take weeks, months, or sometimes years.

The finishing aspect of this procedure also necessitates mutual reconnoitering to foresee what forms and shapes the problem may take in the future. Are there variations that might need to be addressed? Are there previously unforeseen ways in which the problem might sneak up, and what are its warning signs? Creative problem solving is sometimes required in order to determine a new context within which it may need to be managed in a different way. For example, with Leslie's and Marty's management plan, visiting other homes as guests requires careful planning. If friends or relatives have two guest rooms, they use them. If they don't, they make plans to stay in a nearby motel, always with two double beds, never one king-size bed.

At this point, a celebration may be in order. Do something fun together, or spend some time alone, or do both.

In summary, in finishing the process:

1. You recognize that you feel connected again.
2. You know your solution and/or management package.
3. You reconnoiter for future warnings and variations of the problem.
4. You commit to apply your solutions or management package actions.
5. You celebrate.

Does all this process solve a particular problem forever? No such luck. Time passes, people change, and new limitations may be imposed by age, illness, and all sorts of different circumstances. So old problems previously addressed might need to be readdressed as time goes on.

You try this, you try that, and you keep coming back to the same kinds of conversations, lovingly, respectfully, steadily deepening as you go, with a growing repertory of methods that work better than others, and bright ideas that don't work. Not only does your repertory of workable approaches grow, so does your repertory of skills for lovingly and respectfully talking together. As your repertories grow, so too does your sense of safety with one another and with the relationship; so does your trust and confidence in yourself, your partner, the relationship and the tools that you are accumulating and sharpening.

Your flights to Powerland become less and less frequent. On the occasions that they occur, you become increasingly competent and confident in your ability to get into your boat and row it back to Loveland.

It is like any skill that you learn in sports or your trade or profession; you work at it until you become a pro- that is, totally reliable. In this aspect of your life, what you are working on is your capacity to be successfully reliable to yourself and in relationship with another human being. When problems come up, you become reliable in your ability to address them. You become a pro in your capacity to deal with the "big deals" in relationships. If you ski or golf, you may remember a first slope that seemed intimidating or how shooting par seemed impossible. The most important thing is hanging in there, practicing, and developing your heart skills until you become a pro.

And remember, you and your partner, if he or she is involved in working on these skills also, may not master these skills at the same pace. It's like when you don't have simultaneous orgasms. Manage it in the same way, by helping yourself and your partner along with care and tenderness.

CHAPTER FOURTEEN

IF THERE HAS BEEN MALICE

In the previous chapters, we have laid out the skills and procedures necessary for addressing problems up to this point. They are:

1. Remind yourself that you are a volunteer.
2. Rev up your commitment to absence of malice.
3. Commit to continuous connection; identify the disconnect.
4. Set boundaries as appropriate and necessary.
5. Unpack; tell the story. Remember to practice Connected Curiosity.
6. Identify the type of situation you are dealing with: disappointment, interruption, inconvenience, irreconcilable difference, or some combination of the four.
7. Address as outlined in Chapters Nine through Eleven.
8. Finish, as outlined in Chapter Thirteen.
9. Keep practicing. Get better at it.

All the above processes apply, unless there has been malice. If in the process of unpacking and telling our stories it turns out that one partner has *intentionally* done something to hurt the other, they need to get on their knees and beg forgiveness. This is *not* a time for negotiation; it is a time for absolution. Once you act from malice, or use Powerland techniques, you confess and seek absolution.

Sometimes in the early days of working things out, malice can seem to be unconscious, out of our control. Relationships at their best (and we might add at their hardest) force consciousness upon us. When we are single, when we live alone, we often don't get ourselves into the "close quarters" that a live-in relationship imposes on us. We have more space and time alone to regroup after an unpleasant experience, to figure out how to say things nicely. We squelch the impulse to hurt when it comes up, because it just doesn't come up as often.

Intimacy and a live-in relationship place us in a situation in which our Powerland committee members pop up, and pop out, at unexpected moments. Suddenly, we find our mouths popping open and snakes and toads are hopping out! Intimacy at its best forces us to be more conscious. The more conscious we get, the fewer malice-spawned events are going to happen.

Malice is never really unconscious. We can tell when we really wanted to hurt our partner. We find ourselves thinking or saying things like, "I just wanted you to hurt like I did," or "I wanted to teach you a lesson," or variations of those kinds of thoughts. Malice is intentional. You can't have it be intentional and unconscious. When a committee member intentionally hurts a partner, unless you have a Multiple Personality Disorder, you know that it is happening. You join that part of yourself even if minimally, in not stopping, and sometimes in gleeful, sadistic malice. So, it is always conscious.

In a relationship, in a disconnect, someone can be neglectful or ignorant and thus cause harm, but they can't be unconsciously malicious. "Unconsciously malicious" is an oxymoron. This is part of the common law. Acting with malice falls in the spectrum of criminal acts. Criminal acts happen with intention.

As soon as you become aware that you intended harm, you need to go for absolution. This is no time to hedge the truth. You have already betrayed a trust by acting in malice. That betrayal only deepens if you hedge, twist the truth, or make excuses for your behavior. Examples of excuses are statements such as, "I was feeling a lot of stress," or "You really got to me." You must own it up front and in a straightforward way. Then you must honestly and sincerely apologize. This is no time for negotiation; this is no time for problem solving and mutually arriving at some solution or management plan.

The choices are not pretty here. You can stay in Powerland and not apologize, or you can get down on your knees and beg forgiveness. Groveling is in order. Unless you are with someone who cares very little about themselves (and who wants to be with someone like that?), *your failure to do this means an eventual end to the relationship.* Begging forgiveness is the only possibility for getting back to Loveland.

After begging forgiveness, you must do what is necessary to make sure that acting in malice in the way you have done **never** happens again. You must promise yourself and you must promise your partner that it will never happen again. And this must be a promise that you and your partner know can be kept. You may need to do a lot of work with your inner committee. If a malicious act happens twice, you should probably high-tail it to counseling.

At a time like this, it is important to remember your over-arching goal. Do you want a relationship? Do you want to live in Loveland? Or do you want to live in Powerland, grow old alone, lonely, hard, bitter, and disconnected?

So, if and when you become aware that you have acted in malice:

1. Initiate contact with your partner as soon as possible.
2. Honestly confess.
3. Apologize profusely. Grovel.
4. Promise that you will never do that again.
5. Make a plan that ensures that you will keep your promise.
6. Practice self-control. Remember, there are circumstances in your work life in which you have held your tongue and acted carefully and without harm, in order to preserve your job. Your marriage is at least as important. Practice humble self-restraint. Pack Duct Tape (for your mouth).

About Shitburgers

Malice has no place in a significant relationship. None of the Powerland players, none of the warriors, has a place in relationship. They belong on a battlefield, and relationship should never be a battlefield.

Here is a story from when Marty was working with prisoners. One day, a prisoner who had been denied some privilege that required one week's good behavior came to Marty and said, "Well, Doc, if I act good six and one-half days a week, then that ought to be good enough."

Marty said, "I've got a series of questions for you. Just answer them."

"Okay," replied Earl, the prisoner.

"I give you a sandwich. It is 90% beef, 10% shit. Is it a beefburger or a shitburger?"

"Easy, Doc. That's definitely a shitburger."

"It's 99% beef, 1% shit; beefburger or shitburger?"

"Shitburger."

"It's 99.9% beef, .1% shit. Would you eat it?"

"No."

"Then you understand. No shit."

Shitburgers are different than the soy-extended burgers we described earlier. Any little bit of shit in a burger makes it a shitburger. You should not eat shitburgers, and you should not expect your partner to eat a shitburger. Ongoing malice, even a little, has no place in a loving relationship. If you are acting with any malice in an ongoing way, you need to do whatever you need to do to stop it. If you are living with someone who repeatedly acts from a place of malice, you need to get out. Staying only prolongs the agony for each of you. It prolongs the agony for your partner because deep inside, they know they are being bad, and no matter how dishonest they are being about it, they still know. It really feels bad to be a shit, and it really feels bad to be dishonest about it. Not taking a stand only prolongs your partner's being a shit and delays the day on which they will decide to do something about it. In the meantime, you are also suffering. So, refuse to eat shit!

CHAPTER FIFTEEN

SELF-SOOTHING

Here is the moment: The train wreck has happened and a disconnect has occurred. You are still attached. You may be married, you may be committed, and you may be living together. In any case, you are emotionally dependent on this person at whom you are staring, probably with a glare in your eye. Inside, you have whooshed to Powerland.

You have no idea how to understand the problem from their point of view. Your point of view is part of the problem. So you do not know how, whether, or when you are going to get back to Loveland, and you don't know what it is going to cost if you do. Despite your warriors' various protestations that you *never* want to go back there, that it's *not* worth it, the better part of you wants to get back to Loveland.

You don't know what the solution is, how you are going to figure it out, and if what you figure out is going to work or not. You don't know *any* of those damn things! It's like you are in a three-legged race with your partner. You want to break loose and run, or you want to slug them. But each of you still has one leg in the sack together.

It is much harder for men to be in this position, because as a man, you are trained to be in Powerland, to get competitive, to think that what you want is better than what anybody else wants. You think something like, "Wouldn't it just be easier if she would do what I say, do what I want?" This is the temptation of being in Powerland.

The Powerland negotiation skills go something like this: "I'm going to try as much as possible, to give you as little as possible of what you want, and then I get the rest. I'm going to get what I want, and what is left, if anything, is yours. We aren't going to try to get to a mutual 'Yes,' we are going to get to MINE!" And if you have learned how to be a hard negotiator, as most men have, you do your best to deal with this "crooked supplier of love" with whom you happen to be in relationship. They're not delivering on time what you want! Let's see how we can get this thing working again the way I want it. Isn't it like fixing the car? How about we take out a part here, add a part there? You're in Powerland! That's the temptation, in terms of the skills you already have in place.

It's no wonder this position is so tempting. Most guys, and alphas especially, are well-schooled in Powerland language but are deaf, dumb, and blind in the language of emotions. Who wouldn't want to choose a winning hand, spoken in a language in which you are well-versed, as opposed to wandering around in some land where you are deaf, dumb, and blind?

It's not pleasant. What we are asking you to do is like learning to dance on a battlefield, where you are tempted to say, "Dance?! Let's just hunker down and *shoot* something!" Sometimes that shooting will be like a silent sniper; you'll just stick to facts and logic while figuring out how you're going to get yours. In these situations, your partner may experience confusion and hurt. Everything makes sense from a logical perspective, but your partner feels like she is being shot in the gut, because inherently she knows your attempt to reconnect is insincere.

This situation is not easy for you. And to make it worse, it appears, and probably is, much easier for *her*. She's in touch with her feelings, she talks easily, and it feels unfair; you have to work extra hard. She's babbling on endlessly. You feel like you're in a *minefield* and you're supposed to be practicing chivalry! You're supposed to be romping around all the time, like on a dance floor, learning how to gracefully not get blown up, while carrying this babbling bitch around on your shoulders so she won't get harmed. At this moment, that's the last thing you want to do! If you aren't going to practice chivalry, you consider the other choice: Maybe I could just roll the bitch across the minefield and see what blows up! Wouldn't that be easier?!

But you want to live in Loveland. Here is where self-soothing is necessary. What is self-soothing? It is like jerking off and other things that make you feel better. Different people do it differently. It depends on what you believe in and what works for you. Here are some ways that help.

Deep Breathing, Time Out, and Calming Activity

If you are afraid that you will say or do something you really regret, a time-out can give you space to soothe yourself. Use of time-outs should be contracted with your partner before a disconnect, that is, it should be an agreed-upon ground rule. The contract should include:

> A signal: Hands perpendicular, like a referee calling time at a ballgame is a common one.
>
> Length of time: Twenty minutes will often do. If you need longer, say so when you call the time-out.

A check-in should be part of the agreement. A check-in does not mean getting back together; it means that you will report your readiness or lack of readiness to begin the reconnection process. When you check-in, whether in person or by phone, you can tell your partner that you need more time, or that you are ready to talk. If you need more time, you should indicate to your partner how much, and agree to check back in at the end of that time.

It is very important that you call the time-out only for yourself, never for your partner. Calling a time-out for your partner will only incense them. Besides, "scrupulously couching your time-out as your issue has the distinct advantage that no one can argue with you about it (Real, 2007, p.106)."

One of the most powerful self-soothing tools that we have is our breath. Simply taking long, deep, slow breaths can often calm those internal Warriors that are chomping at the bit to be let loose. We can do this while remaining in conversation, or if need be, we can take a time-out and breathe and do the other things recommended in this chapter. During a time-out, breathing deeply for three to five minutes is an amazing self-soother. We suggest deeply inhaling through the nose and then exhaling through the mouth.

Doing an activity that relaxes us and gives us time to think is another way to self-soothe. Many of us have had the experience of being on the verge of saying something we regret to our boss or a business colleague, and saying instead, "Let me have a little time to think about this; I'll get back to you." Then we go for a long walk, or go fishing, or go home and work in the shop or rake leaves. You can do the same with your partner. During these calm-down activities you have a good opportunity to breathe deeply, to remember your affection for your partner and to think about what you want to say and how you want to say it, as well as to picture yourself listening to your partner with connected curiosity.

These activities should be part of a declared time out with your partner. They are a reprieve, to help you avoid saying or doing things you will regret while preparing yourself to reconnect. They should not be used as an escape in the service of avoiding reconnection.

Comparisons

Some guys find terrible comparisons soothing. For example, saying to yourself, "I could be in a much worse situation," or some variation of that theme sometimes helps. You can think about the guy whose wife is a drunk, or the lonely old guy down the street. You remember Nietzsche's words, "That which does not kill us makes us stronger." So, you can say something like, "Well, I'm not dead yet, so I guess I'll go try getting stronger. Let's practice tiptoeing through the mine field again!" Reminding yourself of the progress you have made also helps.

Honoring Your Promise

This form of self-soothing often works well for those who have a spiritual life. You remind yourself that you are doing the right thing by hanging in there, and by keeping your promise. Remember, this is a promise you made to *yourself* first, and then to your partner. You promised yourself that you wanted to learn the skills necessary to live in Loveland; your partner trusts you to keep that promise. There may be children involved.

You soothe yourself by reminding yourself that you are doing the right thing in God's eyes, others' eyes, or according to your own values, standards, and beliefs. You remind yourself that hanging in there is doing the right thing. You don't always know why you are hanging in, but you are hanging in. You give it over to a higher power, reminding yourself that you made your promise and by God, you are going to keep it! You are honoring a commitment, based on a promise. You keep hanging in there, even during tough times, even when you want to eliminate her. You hang in there to learn to use skills and tools which lead you to more joy and more *continuous* connection. While there are times when you want to leave, the times of joy and connection deepen and lengthen.

Honoring a commitment based on this kind of promise is different from living a chronically miserable life while honoring a commitment based on duty, obligation, or responsibility. If you are in this kind of situation, you are living on the drama triangle. If you find yourself wishing that you might die of natural causes before the marriage kills you, you are living on the drama triangle.

Roadmaps and Skills Manuals

Another way to keep yourself soothed and on course is to read books like this one about relationship skills, written by credible professionals. Learning to live in Loveland can be like finding yourself in a foreign country, lost and in the dark, with signs in a language that you can't read. But you've got the guidebook. "Well, the geography I'm looking at right now looks like this picture," you might say. You have to trust the guidebook and soothe yourself by saying something like, "Well, other people have gotten there using this damned guidebook. I'm just as good as they are, so I guess I can get there too! I don't know how the hell I'm going to win this, but I'm not quitting either!" Guys do this in sports and in their work all the time. It also works while mastering relationship skills.

Fear

Fear can be a great motivator and soother, especially for members of an alpha-alpha pair. As Pat and her sister, Mary, were telling the story of their fight, Mary laughed as she shared a thought she had in their night of anguish as she was gathering courage to lovingly go back and reconnect with Pat. "I kept thinking, I sure don't want *her* for an enemy! I gotta do what I need to reconnect, because I want her on my team!" This fear must not be used as motivation for adaptation, but rather for courage to maintain real reconnection.

Mentors and Reference Groups

Other individuals and groups can help provide self-soothing and support for hanging in there and for learning new skills. Some guys do better hanging in a relationship when they have someone or a group they can go to when the going gets rough.

And remember, consulting with others should never turn into a talk session in which your partner gets bashed. If one of your people resources begins to encourage this, unless through the process you become aware that your partner is actually engaging in malice, you should find a different friend, counselor, or group.

Your focus, when contacting these resources, should be on what *you* can learn and how you can improve your relationship skills. Your focus can also be on sharing your pride when you overcome your urges to resort to Powerland behavior and choose instead the more difficult Loveland route. Talking with others can also be used as "confession time," in which you share your embarrassment about unskilled behavior and get support to do the hard work of apologizing to your partner.

Affirmations and Visualization

Affirmations are things we say to ourselves, to help us keep on our path and committed to our promises to ourselves and our partner. Our brain is a very powerful friend and pal. When we engage our mind's power to visualize and become present with ourselves, we soothe ourselves. Some of the self-soothing techniques discussed earlier have inherent self-soothing affirmations. We list them here, along with others:

> If other guys can learn to do this shit, so can I.
>
> I'm not dying. I'm alive and I just feel lost because I'm not accustomed to Loveland language.
>
> I'm not dying; I'm getting stronger.
>
> I'm doing a really good thing for myself and my partner by hanging in there and working this stuff.
>
> I'm a winner for learning this stuff, even though it's hard.
>
> Surrender. Trust. Do not turn away from Love. Go for the Love.

Sometimes visualizing yourself in the arms of someone who is very comforting can help. It might be in the arms of a loving parent, or even your partner. You might imagine holding yourself and soothing yourself to sleep. While using affirmations or visualization, you should see and hear yourself and any other internal comforting person as fully as possible. That increases your mind's effectiveness in self-soothing. You may have already used techniques such as these to help you in your job performance or your golf game.

Soothing You Is Not Your Partner's Job

Some guys make the mistake of expecting their partner to soothe them out of Powerland spaces or scared places. You don't get to do that. She may be soothing herself, she may be trying to figure out where her boundaries are, or, unfortunately, she may be recovering from your latest unskilled volley from Powerland. You don't get to ask her to hold you while she is in the midst of her own side of the journey. To do so is insensitive to her process.

The most help you should expect from your partner in this situation is that she is not being abusive herself. She is helping you if she is doing whatever she needs to be doing in order to act in absence of malice.

A man who seeks this kind of soothing from his partner while she is busy working to find her own truth, or working to recover from a volley or to figure out her boundaries, is a man who is seeking something like a heroin fix. You are seeking a false and temporary fix. Embedded in your search for soothing from your partner in this way is the hidden Powerland hope that she will put her needs aside and instead, take care of you. You are hoping that she will change, or not be herself, or not take care of herself, and give you what you want.

It seems so *easy* for her! She's saying, "Look, we've got this little problem. Let's figure it out." And you think to yourself, "Little?! It's damned World War Three, or a Geneva Summit! Shit! Because of her, I have to walk through that damned minefield again!" You wish she would forget the whole thing and go to bed with you and make love and hold you. Oh yeah, and then maybe you could even watch a ball game on television. You may even try to distract her into doing these things.

If you are a woman in this situation, your job is to hold your ground firmly, and in connection, speak your own truth. If instead you buy into his pleas for you to soothe him in various ways (sometimes called "soothing the male ego"), you worry that he will forget, or artificially assume that everything is okay. You are right; he is likely to forget or assume that everything is okay. You are not helping the relationship. Additionally, you are participating in furthering your own silence, your own absence of voice.

Self-soothing is not supported by conventional male thinking because as a guy, maybe you've had a rough day out there helping to earn the living, and you've been taught that if you've been a good boy, you will get home and mommy will soothe you and take care of you. Or you buy into the traditional model of marriage in which you earn the money and deserve to be taken care of at the end of the day. Well, she has had her day too, even if she has been home all day. She needs for you to be able to take care of yourself; therefore, self- soothing is crucial. Soothing with alcohol or sex, or the distractions of flipping the remote on the television are not going to provide safety.

You must thoroughly commit to the notion that you can hold yourself and soothe yourself and rock yourself to sleep. You commit yourself to walking through that minefield again and again, even when you are not doing it very well. Eventually, you will do it well.

CHAPTER SIXTEEN

ABOUT REGRESSION

We all regress under stress. Regression by definition means "back to the same old thing." Sometimes we can work and work on making all these new changes, and then find ourselves, to our chagrin, participating in destructive Powerland behaviors we thought we had overridden long ago. How does a reformed, committed, signed-on alpha become a Powerland Idiot? The usual suspects show up:

Alcohol
Drugs
Sleep deprivation
Fatigue
Over-scheduling
Over-committing

When we become over-scheduled and over-committed, or get too pushed in goal-oriented tasks, we begin to abuse our partner in the same way we are abusing ourself. We are in danger of doing this also if we perceive that our partner is working right along beside us in a goal-oriented way, perhaps toward some mutually-established goal, such as building a new home. In those occasions, we can fall back onto alpha male team play rules: Suck it up and keep going.

If any one or two non-coach members of the committee take center-stage, they will see things only through their narrow focus and perennial goals. The Warrior will try to exert power over our partner. The Nerd Scientist will express understanding without proper action. The Adaptive/Scared Child will engage in avoidance.

In such cases, you will act like an idiot. That is to say, you will distort reality to fit the confines of a single player's world view, values, goals, and methods.

The idiot, knowing only what it knows, and without an overview of what it doesn't know (which is why we rely on a coach for the overview) will persist in destructive behavior, even in the case of repeated failure. That makes you an idiot.

Give all your trusted Loveland companions instructions on how to tell you to take a timeout. Practice turning on a dime, in circumstances where you don't understand why you are being asked to take a time-out, when you don't agree that you need a time-out, and you don't like being stopped.

CHAPTER SEVENTEEN

HOW TO CHOOSE A MATE, OR, HOW DO I FIND SOMEONE WHO WILL DO THESE STRANGE THINGS WITH ME?

For those readers who are partnerless at this time, a period of self-reflection is necessary before you start looking for a mate. First, ask yourself if you are ready to make a committed, principled, long-term commitment to another human being. By "principled commitment," we mean a commitment to yourself to abide by a code of principles that we have outlined in this book, including a commitment to never act in malice and to make the relationship a priority in your life. There may be other aspects of your life that are important to you, perhaps as important as your relationship. Sometimes you will need to juggle time and energy among these cherished aspects of your life. But when the relationship is in crisis, it must take a front seat. If you are not ready to make this commitment, to yourself and to a potential life partner, then seek a playmate, not a mate.

Examine yourself honestly to see whether **any** of the relationship destroyers you have allowed into previous relationships are still able to sabotage your next relationship chance. Ask trusted friends for feedback on this issue. Assess how you are at work. Are there any of the behavioral liabilities such as those spelled out in *Alpha Male Syndrome* (Ludeman and Erlandson, 2006)? If there is any hint that you still have parts not in control that could menace the relationship, work on this, either with yourself, with trusted friends, or with a therapist. While you may have many good parts of yourself, such as intelligence, humor, kindness when you are not under duress and other desirable traits, if your coach is not in control of alpha liability behaviors, those uncontrolled parts of you, not your positive traits, will determine the outcome of your next relationship. Remember, even if 80% of what you do works well, the 20% that doesn't work well is enough to sabotage the relationship. *Work on this until you are confident that you and your coach are fully in charge of you.*

Pick someone you find interesting and who enhances your time together. A good question to ask yourself is: Is my life fuller, richer, more interesting, more fun and less lonely as a result of my being in relationship with this person? Your life **will** be more challenging, and intimacy will bring its complexities. An affirmative answer to the above question will help you determine if the complexities and challenges are worth how the relationship enhances your life.

Pick someone you admire and respect, and who admires and respects you. Pick someone who appears to responsibly manage their own life and who is responsive to you. Pick someone who is comfortable with being alone as well as in company; someone who has an interesting individual life. You should have a sense that they are a good person.

Chemistry may or may not be present. Judith Wallerstein, Ph.D. in her book, *The Good Marriage* (1995) addresses four varieties of marriage: Romantic, Companionate, Rescue, and Traditional. Three of these types are compatible with the guidance provided by this book. One type, the traditional role-centered marriage is not.

One type is the romantic relationship. In this relationship, there is a high level of chemistry and romance, especially in the beginning. While it may level off later, the "chemistry" often lasts forever. Couples engaged in a romantic relationship, in addition to being held together strongly by attraction and chemistry, may express their feelings passionately, but still in the responsible ways that we have outlined in this book.

The second variety is the companionate relationship, in which the partners are good companions for each other and work well as a team. In a companionate relationship, sexual attraction may bloom more slowly and secondary to the solid establishment of companionship and teamwork. A companionate relationship by no means has to be void of sexual passion. Sexual passion and chemistry, however, are probably not the drivers in this relationship.

The third variety of partnership is the rescue relationship. We call this the odd peoples' home. You each realize how few people could possibly mate with you and are endlessly pleased that you found anyone with whom you are compatible.

The fourth variety of partnership is the traditional relationship, in which traditional roles of husband as wage earner and wife as homemaker are adopted. For many conscious people in this day and time, this relationship no longer works.

Some mutual interests are useful, though not necessary, as long as there is a strong mutual interest in making the relationship a priority and on sharing your adventures from your separate activities with each other.

Regardless of the type of relationship you desire or find yourself beginning, trust should be the first criterion, as it is the foundation for any successful long-term intimate relationship. There are seven *trustability criteria*:

1. They do what they say they will do when they say they will do it.

   Using this criterion is often the simplest and least painful way to weed out unsuitable partners in the beginning of the relationship. If they say they will call you for a date on Tuesday and you don't hear from them for three weeks, take notice. If they say they will call on Tuesday and call instead on Thursday with no mention of or apology for not calling on Tuesday, take notice. If they do not follow through on these little things, how can they be expected to be there with you when the going gets rough, even if they have promised they will?

2. They are aware of their thoughts and feelings (sometimes referred to as their *process*) and are willing to share their process with you, particularly as their process pertains to the relationship.

   You look for someone who is aware enough of what they are thinking and feeling about themselves, you, and the relationship and is willing to talk with you about those.

3. They are willing to hear your process.

   Does this person listen to you when you share your thoughts and feelings? Do they ask questions in an interested way? Are they able to reflect your thoughts and feelings back to you in a way that lets you know they understand what you have said? Or do they change the subject when you share difficult-to-say or difficult-to-hear feelings? Do they use most of the conversational space to talk about themselves, while leaving little space or interest for you?

4. They are willing to engage in a mutual process that makes room and space for your thoughts, feelings, stories, wants and desires as well as their own.

   Are they willing to hear you as well as speak their own truth? Can they state and hold both truths accurately? By hold, we mean that they can value your truth, your process, considering it as important as their own. When those truths and/or needs are different, are they willing to engage in the kinds of problem-solving and management that we have addressed in this book that allows each of you as individuals and both of you as a couple to come out winners? Or, if they hear your position at all, are they judgmental about it? Do they frame their own different position and need as superior? That does not bode well for someone's likelihood of engaging in the dialogues we have proposed in this book.

5. They respect boundaries.

   This is another criterion that can be checked out earlier and rather painlessly in the relationship. Do they say they will pick you up at 7 P.M. and then arrive unannounced at 6:30, saying something like, "I just couldn't wait to see you," or, "I got ready early so I decided to come on over." If you are a woman and this happens early in the relationship and when you still have curlers in your hair, it is not appreciated. Or, if you are a man, does she start doing your laundry or reorganizing your kitchen without asking? When you have said twice that you are tired and ready to go home, do they plead with or cajole you, or worse yet, guilt-trip you, to stay out longer? Again, if small boundaries are not respected, it does not bode well for more important boundaries to be respected later.

6. They do not engage in physical or verbal abuse.

   Physical abuse is self-explanatory. Verbal abuse includes name-calling, character defamation and any explicit or implicit attempt to control or threaten you with harm or abandonment.

7. They take responsibility for their part of a problem.

   If there is a problem, do they own and apologize for their part in it? Or do they avoid discussing it if you bring it up or worse yet, blame you and you alone?

While no one is perfect, these criteria should be held to somewhere between 90 and 95% of the time. Physical and verbal abuse should be absent 100% of the time.

Lastly, in looking for a mate, as the relationship progresses, you may suggest that they read this book and others, such as *The New Rules of Marriage (Real, 2007)* and inquire whether they would be willing to work with the principles and guidelines discussed in these books.

Here are people you **should not** choose. Picking one of these guarantees failure:

A Project to Fix: If they aren't fixed enough by now, under their own steam, chances are 100% you aren't going to do it. This one is guaranteed to get you on the drama triangle, first as the rescuer and then, well, you know the rest.

An Impossible Person in "Need of a Master:" You will spend all your time and energy unsuccessfully trying to stay "on top," while they master you with their impossibility. You want an equal, who will meet you.

Someone You Can't Live Without, or Who Can't Live Without You: You will soon find that you cannot live *with* them, either.

A Wild Person Who You Plan to "Tame:" They will eat you for lunch.

When you have chosen someone you believe is a good candidate to take this amazing journey of intimacy with you, remember that most of the good news about each of you is out within the first three to four months of the relationship. Some couples wait this long before having sex, as the "psychic glue" generated by lovemaking often gums up the brain and makes it more difficult to assess the partner's likelihood of being a good mate. After this period, if the positive signs we outlined above are there, and you still feel confident that your coach is in charge, prepare to later learn realities about yourself and your partner that are surprising, usually in negative ways.

Prepare to work through these disappointments, interruptions, odd inconveniences, and irreconcilable differences as directed in this book. Someone once said that we don't love people who are perfect (and there aren't any anyway, including, to our dismay, ourselves!); we love people we know. Getting to know yourself and your partner through the difficulties adds to the patina of a real human intimate relationship and opens the door to deeper love, of them, of yourself, and of your relationship.

Then you will glory in the wonder of a peaceful, loving, productive, endlessly changing, challenging and adaptable partnership. You should know that in a successful long-term relationship, that feel-good hormone, oxytocin, while not secreted in the intense levels of the beginning of the relationship, continues to roll in at a modest and steady level. It also rolls in at high levels after the successful resolution of a scary disconnect. We wish you well.

CHAPTER EIGHTEEN

WHEN TO SEE A THERAPIST

When

You or your partner, or both of you, should see a therapist if:

1. You or your partner cannot follow the directions in this book.

2. You think you are following the directions but find the same problems coming up that you thought were solved.

3. You or your partner is unwilling or unable to follow your own management protocol for an inconvenience and/or irreconcilable difference.

4. You or your partner is experiencing strong attacks of negative emotion, such as rage, anxiety, bleakness, depression or shame, that do not resolve well by reconnecting.

5. Your partner strongly feels that therapy is necessary in order for the two of you to maintain connection.

6. You and/or your partner experience persistent bafflement about one or more recurrent issues.

Who to See and How to Find Them

Often a good way to find a competent therapist is to talk with other couples who have successfully navigated couples therapy. You may want to have an exploratory session with one or more therapists before settling in with one. If you have never been to therapy and feel some disdain for therapy, but you have been in so much pain you decide to give it a try, there is a big pitfall to beware of. There are three levels of therapist effectiveness: a therapist who does harm; a mediocre therapist who does no harm but does not help; an effective therapist. If you should perchance go to one of the first two initially, *do not give up hope*. Do not assume that all therapists are either incompetent or harmful. Keep looking.

Look for a therapist who is experienced in connection-oriented couples work. Be aware that you and/or your partner will initially work hard at being in charge of the therapy and subordinating the therapist. A competent therapist will fearlessly and yet gently face one or both of you. A good therapist will not try to "rope" you into therapy, but rather non-judgmentally present you with your choices and the likely outcomes of those choices. You will get a sense of being helped. You will feel some sense of relief. You should have a sense of respect for the therapist that you choose.

While a good therapist will encourage each partner to speak their truth, you should also get a sense that the therapist is willing to support the relationship, unless it is a chronically abusive one.

Goal

The goal of the therapy that you will want is for you and your partner to be able to reliably maintain continuous connection and reliably know how to make suitable repairs when a disconnect occurs.

To this end, a good therapist will be astute in helping you to identify disconnects, establish appropriate boundaries, unpack your stories, problem-solve around disappointments and interruptions, and come up with a management plan for inconveniences and irreconcilable differences. If either or both of you have childhood injuries that render this difficult for you, a competent therapist will help identify this and treat it, or refer you to treatment elsewhere. Ideally, these childhood issues will be addressed within the context of the couples' therapy and will add to the deepening love and understanding between you and your partner.

When to Fire a Therapist

1. If either of you dislike, distrust, or disdain the therapist.

2. If therapy sessions are often non-illuminating and/or not supportive of your efforts to maintain connection.

3. If anything feels creepily unacceptable. This might include a therapist who flirts with one of you, is chronically late for appointments, changes fees without notice, or doesn't return phone calls.

4. Do not take referrals from a therapist you fire. However, if the therapist you are seeing should openly disclose that they do not think they can help you, you may want to ask for a referral.

If the above conditions do not apply, if you have a sense that the therapist knows what she or he is doing and that your discomfort has to do with your response to needing to change, hang in there. It's good to remember that it was you who came with the problem, not the therapist.

CHAPTER NINETEEN

ABOUT COMMITMENT AND REASONS NOT TO PRACTICE THESE SKILLS (AND STAY A TOTAL FUCKING ASSHOLE FOR THE REST OF YOUR LIFE)

About Commitment

The commitment to Loveland means 100% commitment to never use power plays in the relationship; to never use power plays at, on, or over your partner. The commitment means that when one or both of you use power plays and it is noticed, that it is a crisis; everything stops, and the crisis plans that we have spelled out begin. The outcome of the crisis plan is a mutually understood version of the problem and a solution or management strategy that does not include any power over the other person. If one or both of the partners consciously refuse, in the presence of clear understanding of what they are doing, to relinquish paranoia-driven survival and self-protective strategies in the relationship, then the remaining partner, if still committed to living in Loveland, must gather their power to terminate the relationship, because they do not have a partner. They have someone who wants to play at being a partner except when it doesn't suit them. To decide to stay in a relationship with someone who is faking being in Loveland is to choose chronic marriage, an abusive situation, or both. Staying in a chronic and/or abusive marriage is to look forward to eating shitburgers for breakfast, lunch, and dinner for the rest of your life.

Otherwise, there really aren't a lot of reasons to not do this process. But first, let's review:

The train wreck *will* come. To know that and to commit to dealing with it is crucial. The skills that we have presented here work. Reading about these skills won't solve everything. Sometimes people know what they are supposed to do but freeze when it comes time to do it. It's like taking skiing lessons; you've done well with the instructor, but you get to the top of the slope and you freeze. The good thing about this process is that you can tell where, when, and how your Loveland connection stops. Remember the signs that we discussed earlier: Feelings in your body such as "icy-hot" in your face, a gnawing in your gut, tension in your neck, chest, solar plexus, belly or pelvis; feeling "out of love;" seeing your partner negatively or feeling "distant" from your partner. Pat calls this seeing the relationship and your partner through shit-colored glasses. The process we have detailed is not an obscure process.

The commitment must be in place on each person's part to:

1. Deal together with relationship train wrecks with an absence of malice.
2. Learn whatever can be learned about yourself and the other.
3. Get back to Loveland.

The commitment is to learn whatever is necessary about yourself, your partner, and the relationship so that you become a reliable and safe partner in getting back to Loveland. You learn enough skills to stop yourself when you are tempted to fly to Powerland. You learn enough skills to tell your story and to listen to your partner's story. You learn enough skills to recognize disappointments, interruptions, or inconveniences and irreconcilable differences, as well as their endless variations and combinations. You become adept at problem solving and managing differences. You don't have to be perfect, just good enough. And you really have already learned to use your highest levels of skill in your workplace and in team sports.

About Ambivalence

Some alpha males and most beta males intrinsically want to be in connection and will have that positive commitment. However, most alpha males are ambivalent about connection. It often feels like it isn't worth it, it's not do-able, and you can think of a lot of other guys who will reassure you that relationships just don't work, they are just too hard. Every alpha person has a place inside of themselves where they feel they are a survivor of the enmity of others, where the choice is to be predator or prey. In this survival place, love is the problem, not the solution. This place kicks up in relationship when the going gets tough. Ambivalence happens. Not only are you deaf, dumb and blind, you feel ambivalent about learning to play pinball!

The deaf, dumb, and blind guy who learned to play the mean pinball had to learn to do it by *feel*. If you want to immigrate to Loveland, if you don't want to live the years left to you in this life cold, hard, bitter and alone, just as if you move to a geographical foreign country, you have to feel your way, you have to learn the language and the customs and the geography of your new home. Of course you wonder at times if the move was worth it! Of course you miss your old home! And of course, you feel as if you are navigating in the darkness.

Here are the common excuses for failing at maintaining continuous connection:

Not Enough Courage

Self-soothing requires courage. To gird your loins and walk through that minefield when you would rather do something else takes courage. To walk through that minefield again and again when you are not doing it very well takes courage. There are so many other ways in which you enjoy your competence. To fumble at learning skills at which you are not adept takes courage.

Laziness

Laziness is another reason not to practice these skills. Marty tells the following story about an actual dialogue that happened with an alpha male, Ralph (not his actual name), who was being coached in these techniques by Marty. Ralph kept coming up with one excuse after another to not practice these skills.

> Finally, Marty says, "We know from other contexts in your life that you are capable of using higher levels of skills. You said you loved this person. You said you were committed. You said you wanted this relationship to work. And you purposefully go about using shitty, incompetent, and useless techniques in your relationship when you know better? What the hell kind of logic is that?"
>
> "Well, I don't like it that you frame it that way," replies Ralph.
>
> Marty isn't letting him off the hook. "So, make another frame. How is it you are going to use your highest level of skill from this day forward?"
>
> "Well, I haven't committed to *that* yet."
>
> "Well, what are you committed to? Nothing? You just bullshittin'? You spending money here to just bullshit?"
>
> "Well, always using my highest level of skill would be *work*!"
>
> "So, failure is better than work?
>
> "No."

"Well, failure is guaranteed. Work is not. It might work, and it might not. Using techniques you know won't work guarantees failure. Is that easier in your mind, to know that you are a certain failure? Or would you like to take a little risk here?!"

"Well, now that you put it that way. . . . "

We expect our partner to change. We expect our partner to work hard when we are not working hard, or when we are working hard in the wrong ways. We don't like, and therefore avoid, the risks of fumbling where we feel inadequate, or of seeking help from someone who can coach us.

Another client of Marty's said, "I do it in my office for money. God-damn if I'm going to use my highest skills at home. That's where I'm supposed to relax!"

"You do it in your office for money but you're not going to do it at home? Then, how is it supposed to work?"

The client goes off into his tirade about how she's supposed to change.

"So, you're committed to using this lousy level of skills at home, to see if she really loves you? I'm going to tell you something. Whether she loves you now or not, she'll eventually not love you and you won't have to continue this trial; I'll tell you how it works out. You can test it, if you want."

"How can you be so sure it won't work at home?"

"You can find out how I can be so sure, or you can use your highest level of skill."

Loss of Heart

If you are with a partner who is repeatedly out-of-the-ballpark difficult, you may lose heart. If you are with someone who is willing to act with malice, you must leave.

Sometimes you will hook up with someone who is dependent, financially or otherwise, and once your partner gets more on their feet, or the children are grown, or for other reasons, you find out that you just don't have the heart to be with this person for the rest of your life. In this case, the words to that old song, "There ain't no good guys, there ain't no bad guys, there's just you and me and we just disagree," are appropriate. You can leave without trashing the other. Jane Fonda said it elegantly about her past husbands: "I had a number of husbands and marriages, each of which lasted a number of years, and each was just perfect for that time in my life." She spoke from her heart; they were all good people. "There ain't no good guys, there ain't no bad guys...."

Terrence Real advises (Real, 2007):

> If there are no children involved, whenever you feel, despite the pain and turmoil that will ensue, that you have no interest in your partner and won't have any no matter what he does, then it's unfair not to set him free to go find someone else who will cherish him. If there are children involved, you should part when you feel you really have no other option (p.270).

If self-soothing fails, if your level of interest and your priorities cannot maintain whatever systems you have put in place to make the relationship work, when you have sought therapy to no avail, or if your partner will not participate in working on a relationship that is intolerable to you, you may bow out. But the bowing out does not mean that the other person is a bad guy. Both of you entered the relationship without malice, and proceeded without malice. The relationship should be ended without malice. Words to the effect of "I can't manage myself well enough" or "I've decided this is too much for me" are appropriate here. Owning your own choice is the responsible thing to do.

Otherwise, there really aren't lots of reasons to stop learning and working this process. If you find someone to whom you are attached, and you care about them, and if they attach to you and care about you, you are now in the three-legged race situation. What else can you do except proceed with the process? As one of our friends Michael, a fisherman, says about proceeding, "If you caught it, you clean it."

Here is an excerpt, written by one of Marty's successful clients, a medical doctor. The title is his:

Stupid Alpha Male's Disease

If you are an alpha male looking for Loveland or a way out of Powerland and have finished this book, you may be suffering from Stupid Alpha Male's Disease (SAMD). If you have recently left a long-term relationship (like a 30 year marriage), if you "still love her, but you are not in love with her," if you thought the problem was irreconcilable differences (before you read *Winning at Love* that is), you probably have SAMD. You are just not getting out of the relationship what you "need." Right?

Maybe you picked up this book because you found another woman who seems to fulfill your needs, and seems to be leading you to Loveland after a long absence. Or you may have gone head to head with an alpha female for 15 years and you find a beta who eases you to Loveland for real. Or worse, you hook up with an alpha after a life with a doormat (beta without a spine) because this new woman is your intellectual equal, your soulmate, and now you realize that you are still in Powerland. You probably have SAMD.

It is likely that sooner or later, unless you follow the principles of *Winning at Love,* the new relationship will become a lot like the one you left. SAMD results from trying to force the strategies of Powerland, strategies having to do with winning, ruling, or controlling the relationship. The artful, successful alpha rarely sees himself as "stupid." The most useful diagnostics in medicine tell the entire story of the disease in a strikingly clear phrase, like heart attack, cancer, or stroke. You understand the nature of the problem with instant clarity when hearing these diagnoses. The same is true for SAMD.

Two general scenarios are common. Either you have reached your goals in Powerland—you have a successful legal practice, high-level management position, or other variations of a successful professional life or trade. Or the opposite may be true. You are disappointed in your career, you are not going to win the Nobel Prize for anything, you don't have any progeny, or if you do, they are estranged. Your search has brought you to this book, and with the hope of learning how to live in Loveland. A cure is possible.

Winning at Love: The Alpha Male's Guide to Relationship Success may help in one of the following two situations. If the long term relationship is "only" on the rocks—there is a separation but not yet a divorce, and the connection is bleeding but not broken, then your best bet may be emergency surgery, using these principles and an experienced surgeon, in this case, a good therapist.

If you or your spouse has killed the marriage, a heart is broken and scars have left it cold, you may be better off with the secretary, the coffee date ("we're just friends"), the coworker or the professional colleague, whose attention has shown you the gates of Loveland. This person has seen your prowess in Powerland and makes you feel special. She (or he) is probably a beta who doesn't realize what they are getting into.

Winning at Love gives you the tools to understand that you are "dis-eased," that is, not at ease, in Loveland. While that realization is a hard pill to swallow, it is the first step to a cure. To prevent a relapse or Whoosh back to Powerland, the remedy for SAMD must come from within, a change in priorities, and a decision to abandon malice.

The concept that irreconcilable differences do not ring the death knell for a relationship is too important not to reiterate. If you volunteer to enter a second relationship with the idea of going about it using only the tools of Loveland, the longer and deeper and closer it gets, the more irreconcilable differences will be uncovered (again).

The basics laid out by Marty and Pat are the best therapeutic regimen for SAMD, particularly the problem of recurrences (jet plane to Powerland). Unfortunately, like other sexually transmitted diseases, only steadfast dedication to vigilance in the fine print of your relationship will prevent relapses of SAMD. As a survivor of SAMD, I know that the only way to stay in Loveland and stay healthy is to abhor malice, treat your partner's actions as innocent until proven guilty, and then perhaps most important, practice, practice, practice.

EPILOGUE

INFINITE DIALOGUE AND ADVANCED WORKBOOKS

Making a commitment to be in a relationship is making a commitment to be in infinite dialogue. Why? Because role-centered relationships are passé in the cosmopolitan world. All good relationships are now process-centered. You can't make it in a relationship by just doing your roles right. The "your job is to nurture my ego while I financially support us and protect you" relationship just doesn't work. So, you commit to infinite dialogue. Hopefully, you are not repeating a painful dialogue over and over, like the drama triangle that we discussed earlier. Each member in a couple grows and changes over time, and there will always be new problems to solve and new situations to manage.

Marty speaks of his long dialogue with Leslie that took place over one-and- one-half years before they worked out something about bedtime, a core irreconcilable difference between them. Marty says, "When I and my New York self visited with Leslie's family in Minnesota, I had some ideas about the Midwest and people from the Midwest, but I didn't have a working understanding of the mechanics of someone coming from Minnesota and the specific ratchets and gears and stuff and why things go in the order they go and what's permissible. And when you are not comfortable, the tendency is, you want to take a gear out. We don't need this gear! (Laughs) If you don't know how the damn thing works, you don't know if you can take the damn thing out! All you think is, 'This thing is squawking; get rid of it!' The infinite dialogue is about figuring out what makes you, your partner, and the relationship work."

David, a retired engineer and an accomplished sailor who loves his boat, speaks of relationship like a boat. "When I bought my boat, someone told me that it would take ten years to get to know all the systems on the boat. Well, I figure a relationship is the same way. You can't possibly understand a relationship overnight. As long as I hang in there and practice, and explore the relationship like the systems on the boat, I should be able to master these skills."

Advanced Workbooks

Even with the mastery of skills, as long as we are in relationship, we keep learning. Just when we think we have it down, some new life situation, or cast of characters, or variations of our Warriors, pops up, like in characters in the video games, to help us to continue to sharpen our skills and learn. Marty and Leslie's recent "Trip to Deadwood" reminds us of that. The following was written by Leslie, in response to an AFGO (you know what that stands for: Another Fucking Growth Opportunity) in their relationship. Here is Leslie's story.

My Trip to Deadwood
By Leslie

I thought we were doing quite well. My sweetheart developed a life threatening bowel obstruction. We got him into the hospital. They did the things they do and he looked better. I went home to sleep a bit.

I awoke to a call from him at 5:30 A.M. "Come and Get Me Out of Here!" was the summons. I went. I got him out of there, after cleaning up the battleground. If you have a colostomy or live with someone who does, then you know what I mean. If you don't, you don't want to know. During some of the desperation he yelled at me. I yelled back to not yell at me. He slammed a door. This was in a hospital, I remind you, and 6:30 A.M.

It took all I had to get him out of there, but it worked. We both signed the Against Medical Advice form. We stole some extra-large hospital gowns (two: you need one for front and one for back). We bypassed all the usual bureaucracy by simply wheeling out to the car.

He said he would never go to a hospital again. I offered to talk with home health nurses to make that so, and he agreed. He has terminal cancer. He should be able to choose where he lives with his cancer. It was a very hard week, in summary. At home he got a tiny bit better each day. I went ahead with my life, which means I did not cancel my next work trip. Meanwhile, I carried a load of fear and dread.

From a hotel room, I called him. He was suddenly OK. He had a good talk with the doctor in charge of his hospitalization. They came to terms and were now best friends. He even had a good talk with the nursing supervisor about how to better train the night staff. What he did not do was to talk with either of them about getting care at home.

I should feel fine but I don't. Somehow my fear and dread just doubled. As we talk, I realize I'm talking with a man who is not my sweetheart. As I try to put words on how bad I feel, his responses become more and more irritable. Who is the guy? Then I hear him say that he is like Al Swearingen in the town of Deadwood – an HBO series about the old West. If you haven't seen it, you don't need to go back through the back-issues of the series to understand. Al stands above the town, alone out on his balcony, and directs the life-and-death problems of the whole town. He answers to no one and has no one, other than the people who do his bidding. My guy on the phone says that he took a hard line to start with (no more hospitals ever) and now is negotiating. Very reasonable sounding, he is.

I can't get over this fear and dread thing. Over the course of a long dark night I come to understand that my sweetheart has been running a desperate war, starting with his first attack of stomach cramps, into bad night nursing care and my subsequent rescue, and ending with the cease-fire when he and the doctor had their chat. When I thought I was being his loving partner, in actual fact I was being his foot soldier, the necessary cannon fodder. Now suddenly this general has said, "Never mind, it's over."

It was mention of Al Swearingen that caused my painful "Oh Shit!" moment. I saw that I had been mistaken about our being loving partners during this episode. This episode was actually a battle, he was in charge, I was not consulted, he was alone, I was alone, it was a war, and power was the focus. No general would have it otherwise.

Once I had the formulation, I wrote it all down so I could remember it, and slept. When I saw him next, we talked it over. He saw what I saw. If he hadn't I couldn't have stayed with him. We both know that. Thanks to all the gods and goddesses and to my sweetheart that we are back to being loving partners now. Next time we will try to watch for that General. If any situation starts to feel desperate, The General will be there, circling. We will watch for the Desperation cue.

Here is Marty's story:

> What a shock. The third draft of this book was almost done and ready to go out to readers for critique. Then I took Leslie on her "Trip to Deadwood." I was clueless. Here I was, the world's leading expert on Alpha males in Loveland and I found myself deaf, dumb and blind one more time. Thankfully, my DUCT TAPE held. I kept quiet, listened well, and was overwhelmed with the clarity and truth of Leslie's tale. I now understand that my male identity is so tied up in being in charge and in control, especially in chaotic circumstances. Think Tommy Lee Jones in *The Fugitive,* taking charge, barking orders to take over the search for the runt looking for the one-armed man. That's me. Battlefield ready. Not good for Loveland. So, I checked out my inventory of guys on my committee at this time in order to forestall further nasty surprises. Lo and behold, the following guys swarmed out of the woodwork when called:
>
>> Warriors I and II, of course, reported to duty.
>>
>> Warrior I/Soldier. In this case, it was the General. When I was in Powerland, working in the prison system, one of my many nicknames was the General. I had believed that the General was not part of my relationship with Leslie. When he was outed by Leslie, he claimed that he had been in charge all along, and had only provisionally committed to my life in Loveland as long as it "worked out." To him, I say, "Fuck you. I am here to stay."
>>
>> The Sly Seducer, a version of the Secret Agent, and described in grotesque detail in Robert Green's book *The Art of Seduction* (2001), showed up and reminded me that there are always greener pastures to plow if this relationship gets to be "too much trouble." To him I say, "Fuck you. I am here to stay."
>>
>> The Rage Rat, a thug version of Warrior I, showed up, saying, "I am only going to put up with so much." To him, I say, "Fuck you. I am here to stay."
>>
>> My nerd Scientist showed up, saying that my time in Loveland was merely an anthropological expedition to further science and was really only for the purpose of increasing my knowledge of the human race. I could leave any time I wanted to. I had to fess up and say that initially, he had been in charge of my coming to this relationship. And now, to him, I say, "Thank you for getting me here, and now, go away. I'm here to stay."

The Adaptive Child showed up, whining and suggesting I lay low and keep out of harm's way. To him I reply, "No, I will comfort you and take care of you, but I am here to stay."

And if the patriarchal stereotype, Father Provider shows up, saying, "I'm paying the bills, so I'm gonna call the shots.", or any other version of that, I will say, "Fuck 'em, I'm here to stay."

There, I felt better after inventorying and responding to each of them.

All incarnations of alpha maleness are intrinsically in Powerland. So, forget smugness. In Wendell Phillip's famous words, "Eternal vigilance is the price of liberty." Thanks to Leslie for keeping me on my toes. Thanks to me for my willingness to engage Duct Tape and to do an inventory and to fess up.

About Surrender

Surrender is about giving oneself fully. It is one of the last skills an alpha learns in life. We are built to survive and lead, not to surrender. Nonetheless, at times, we are just plain wrong about an issue. This story is a good example of how, for years, I thought I had surrendered to continuous connection with Leslie and yet, in a self-proclaimed "emergency," which, if I am honest, was actually a fit of pique about poor nursing care, I blithely let my General take over and did not notice it or initially recognize it when confronted. Suspect your motives if you find yourself fighting for honor, the American way, or the Mother/Fatherland when you partner is working hard at sharing their experience of a problematic situation. With an otherwise trustworthy partner who disagrees with you about the "facts", it is best to consider yourself "guilty until proven innocent," rather than the reverse.

This journey is for the long haul, and is not for the faint of heart. It is like taking off on a *Star Trek* adventure, with the infinity of outer space as the setting, and with all the possible dangers to avoid, recover from, and learn from. As in the *Star Trek* journeys, there is also the infinite beauty and the sense of pioneering and accomplishment.

Marty gets tears of tenderness in his eyes when he speaks of Leslie. He says, "I was deaf, dumb, and blind. In the beginning, and for a long time, I wore out the love of many. And so now, I softly, sweetly appreciate that I have indeed learned to play a mean pinball when it comes to being in relationship, especially as an immigrant from the heights of Powerland."

Martin Gary Groder was a beacon of light to many; sometimes searing light, sometimes warming light, always brilliant light. He died after a long and courageous battle with colo-rectal cancer on October 12, 2007.

This book can be summarized simply:

1. In the absence of malice, the only sources of pain in a relationship are disappointments, interruptions, inconveniences, and irreconcilable differences.
2. If you are an alpha male and you want a continuing connected relationship, do not turn away from love and do not instead go into survivor roles in a crisis. Do not proceed back to ordinary life before reconnecting. No priority is above continuous connection.
3. A relationship is not a shoulder-to-shoulder work team going towards external goals; rather, it is a face-to-face heart connection.

The rockets are firing. Enjoy the journey. Three, two, one, blast-off!

CHEAT SHEET: WHEN A DISCONNECT HAPPENS

1. Remember that you are a volunteer, and so is your partner. You want to be here, you want her there with you, and she doesn't have to stay.
2. Commit to absence of malice. Do what you need to do to honor that commitment. Soothe yourself. Use Duct Tape.
3. Commit to Continuous Connection. Make this an essential priority in your life. While your relationship does not have to be the only priority in your life, when a disconnect happens, reconnecting should take priority over everything else, with the exception of personal physical safety for you, your partner, and your dependents.
4. Set boundaries. Set boundaries around name calling, around defining the problem in a nasty or judgmental way, around time, and around previous voluntary behaviors that are no longer useful.
5. Unpack the disconnecting event; tell the story. LISTEN. Engage in feedback loops until you can tell the story from your partner's perspective and your partner can tell the story from your perspective, and until you both agree with the other about their contributions to the problem.
6. Apologize for harm caused by ignorance or neglect.
7. If you have acted in malice, beg for forgiveness and take action to never repeat malicious behavior. If forgiven, start back at Step 1.
8. If no malice has occurred, determine if the problem is a disappointment, interruption, or inconvenience/irreconcilable difference. Address accordingly.
    a. If the problem is a disappointment, grieve and change your expectations. Make sure your adjustment is one you believe you can live with. If not, keep working.
    b. If the problem is an interruption, make a plan.
    c. If the problem is an irreconcilable difference/ inconvenience, make a management plan.
9. Finish. You will know you have finished when you feel the absence in your body of signals of disconnect and you feel loving and satisfied with your partner, yourself, and the relationship.
10. Self-soothe as necessary at each step. Self-soothing can include deep breathing, taking a break, reminding yourself that if others can do it, so can you, reminding yourself of your commitment and visualizations and affirmations.
11. Repeat.
12. Repeat.
13. Repeat.

RULES OF THE FOUR LANDS AND CHOICES WE HAVE

In 1969, Marty initiated the Asklepieion program at the Marion, Illinois Federal Prison. He began this program from scratch, with no budget, no personnel and no support; a perfect starting place! Initially, the program did not even have a name. The initial participants in the program were volunteers, and not of the highest quality in terms of trainability, character and intelligence, even for prisoners. He needed to have something concrete to offer them; he had to figure out a set of rules that would work to help them change their lives in ways that would feel better to them and make them less dangerous to themselves and others, perhaps even result in their productive release from prison.

Marty's Hebrew name is Moshe, which stands for Moses, so he thinks in commandments. Negative covenants (Thou Shalt Not's), bound in a tradition of right action, are key ingredients if they are held to by top alphas (Reiff, 2007). Marty knew he had to start with some hard-core rules for his treatment of hard-core criminals. He started with the two rules that were intrinsic and successful in the Synanon program. Synanon, invented by Chuck Diedrich, was an initially successful therapeutic community for street junkies using a highly altered version of Alcoholics' Anonymous. Diedrich's most spectacular invention was a part of the Synanon program called "The Game," an extraordinary confrontation group that stood out, even in the hey-day of encounter groups, as the toughest game in town. There were two critical rules in "The Game:"

Commandment	**Comment**
1. No violence, and no threats of violence.	Intimidation is violence or a threat of violence. The purpose of violence or threats of violence in an ongoing relationship is to dominate and exploit the other person.
2. No mind-altering substances.	To this rule, Marty added "...and no mind-altering situations." The current update of this would be "No addictions," because any addiction alters our capacity to relate meaningfully with ourselves and others. This includes sex

addictions, drug addictions, overwork, television addictions, gambling, risk-taking, extreme sports, extreme workouts, and others.

Starting with these two rules, and using his background in Transactional Analysis, Marty asked himself, "What else causes real harm here in a maximum security prison?" That analysis led to the following three rules:

3. No gambling.	Gambling debts lead to corruption and/or death in penitentiaries.
4. No sex with others.	Consensual sex in prison is unusual, and even if one of his volunteers had engaged in consensual sex, a jealous partner may come after him, so it is dangerous.
5. Follow all the rules.	This includes the prison rules, the inmate culture rules and the staff culture rules. You can follow the rules and always get the job done anyway.
6. And no other stupid things.	A stupid thing is something that is done only once out of ignorance, that causes harm to self or others. The first time is ignorance; there is one free pass only. After that, it should never happen again.

Marty's Asklepieion program became a highly successful treatment program for hardcore criminals with hardcore character defects. The recidivism rate among volunteers who participated in the Asklepieion programs who had 18 months or more in program was reduced from 40-60% to 13% (These percentages varied depending on the facility from which the inmate was released.). Recidivism was defined as reincarceration within the two years post-release. The vast majority of recidivism, if it was to occur, occurred within the first two years. This was replicated in similar programs that sprang from this one in a variety of federal and state facilities.

Why was the Asklepieion program so successful? Reiff (2007) makes it clear that authentic charisma, authentic sanctity, grace if you will, is something that we can have when we have a time-honored covenant with consistent "Thou Shalt Not's," that are both internalized and supported by our surrounding community. It is critical that alphas in powerful positions embody these. As Barbra Streisand said in the movie, *Nuts*, "There's nothing more dangerous than an asshole with power." Conversely to Barbra's statement, there is nothing more grace-full than an alpha who embodies and embraces time-honored "Thou Shalt Not's."

With this in mind, Marty has crafted a set of rules for four lands. By the way, there are two other lands, Detachment Land and Orderland, in addition to Loveland and Powerland, which were the two lands that we focused on for the purposes of this book. We will begin Marty's descriptions of and rules for the two other lands:

Detachment Land

The goal and highest value in detachment land is to avoid attachment, to anything or anyone. The Buddha and his followers have developed this area extensively. Here are its rules:

Commandment	**Comment**
1. Do not harm any living being.	
2. Do not attach	
3. Love and respect all.	
4. No addictions; no gods.	
5. Walk without footprints.	This rule was shown well in the old television series, *Kung Fu*. Have no image, no need to leave a legacy. Live on and leave the earth as if the earth never experienced your presence.
6. And no other stupid things.	

Orderland

The highest values in orderland are (guess what?), order, rules and law; not love. Orderland rules are:

Commandment	Comment
1.Do not break the laws of man, nature, and/or god.	
2. Never step over the ethical line.	Even if the government's law allows it.
3. Correct, compensate for, and clean up all breaches quickly.	
4. No addictions	Addicts break the rules, since their addictions become more important than rules.
5. Promote, promulgate and protect the law.	
6. And no other stupid things.	

Powerland

In Powerland, the goal is to be loved by most and feared by all. The highest value is power. Its rules are:

Commandment	Comment
1. Don't hurt anybody by accident; it is too expensive.	All harm should be deliberate, purposeful and with excellent payoff. In order to do this, do not engage in fair fights; fair fights are dangerous because you can lose. Follow Sun Tsu's advice in *Art of War* (1998): Bring overwhelming force to bear on an underwhelming enemy.
2. Trust, but verify.	Machiavelli (1494) says that

alliances are crucial to victory. You can't form alliances unless you trust someone, but you really have to know that they are doing what they are supposed to be doing. Machiavelli also states that alliances are never permanent since they are only for the purpose of achieving your own ends. Fifteen hundred years of Russian paranoia bears this out.

4. No addictions. no vulnerabilities.

Addictions put something ahead of survival.

5. No vulnerability

Vulnerability also puts something ahead of survival. Vulnerability can put fear or love or other disgusting things ahead of survival and power.

5. Don't break the rules unless absolutely necessary.

Risk equals the probability of failure and should not be used as an excitement enhancer.

6. And no other stupid things.

Loveland

Commandment

1. No malice.
2. Stay cleanly connected 24/7.
3. Repair all disconnects.
4. No addictions.
5. Follow the rules. No shortcuts.
6. And no other stupid things.

About Criminals, Bonobos, and Our Alpha Choices

The chimpanzee, found north of the Congo River, is the closest animal species to the human. In the 1920's, a scientist named Robert Yerkes thought that he had discovered a third species, equally kin to the chimpanzee and the human. He named this species Bonobo. They were thought to be a different species because they behave quite differently than chimpanzees.

Chimpanzee tribes are ruled by an alpha male, with usually two or more subordinate alpha males who terrorize, bully and extort food, sex and grooming from other tribe members, including beta and alpha males, females and children. Worse yet, they are known to war neighboring tribes to extermination. When they want to expand their own tribe, they use tools, such as spears (sharpened sticks), or they merely fight with and bite off the testicles of the alphas of the invaded tribe. The alpha males then rape and carry off the female chimpanzees to be incorporated into their tribe. Chimpanzee behavior has been used to justify or explain our human proclivity toward war and other power-valuing behavior.

In contrast are the Bonobos, found south of the Congo River. Their tribes are ruled by older, higher-status alpha females. Beta males and both alpha and beta females are allowed to separate from the mother at around four years of age. The alpha male offspring are kept at the mother's side the longest, not leaving until they are about seven years old. Thus, they are given the longest training in "acting right." When a female wants to leave the tribe, she is allowed by her own tribe to wander off. She then approaches the alpha female of the tribe she wants to join and does the appropriate version of Bonobo request. The mama of the tribe she wants to join says the Bonobo equivalent of, "Yes, dear, and we have a nice young man for you." She then takes the requesting female to one of the tribal males, they have sex, and the female is incorporated into the tribe.

The alpha male has definite roles in the Bonobo tribe. They include protecting the tribe from leopards, scouting out food sources, and alerting and leading the tribe when it is time to move to new eating grounds. If an alpha male attempts to bully and take primacy in the tribe, senior alpha females band together and drive him out of the tribe. Only his groveling permits his return to the tribe.

Disputes and irritations in the Bonobo tribes are resolved by g-g, or genital-genital rubbing. This occurs between males and females, males and males, females and females, and adults and children. Sexual pleasuring occurs inside as well as outside of procreative activity.

More recently, it has been discovered that the Bonobo is not really a separate species from the Chimpanzee. They are simply Chimpanzees who have decided to and learned how to live in Loveland.

If criminals, with characters much more hardened than those of us alphas, can decide to adopt rules that make them happier and more functional and yes, more loving, so can even the toughest alpha. And if Chimpanzees can decide to live in Loveland, not Powerland, so can we.

We hope you choose Loveland.

After all, would you rather your balls be chomped, or rubbed?

REFERENCES

Alberti, Robert and Emmons, Michael. *Your Perfect Right* (Atascadero California: Impact Publishers, Inc. 2005).

Bradley, James and Powers, Ron. *Flags of Our Fathers* (New York: Bantam Books, 2000).

Cohen, Gene. *The Mature Mind: The Positive Power of the Aging Brain* (New York: Basic Books, 2005).

De Waal, Frans and Lanting, Frans. *Bonobo, the Forgotten Ape* (Los Angeles and Berkeley: University of California Press, 1997).

Fisher, Roger and Ury, William. *Getting to Yes: Negotiating Agreement Without Giving In* (New York: Penguin Books, 1991).

Gottman, John. *The Seven Principles for Making Marriage Work* (New York: Three Rivers Press, 1999).

Greene, Robert. *The Forty-Eight Laws of Power* (New York: Penguin, 2000).

Greene, Robert. *The Art of Seduction.* (New York: Penguin Putnam, Inc. 2001).

Gur, Ruben C., Gunning-Dixon, Faith, Bilker, Warren, Gur, Raquel. Sex Differences in Temporo-limbic and Frontal Brain Volumes of Healthy Adults. Cerebral Cortex, September 2002, Vol. 12, No. 9, 998-1003.

Karpman, Stephen. *Transactional Analysis Journal,* 1969. "The Drama Triangle."

Kiecolt-Glaser, Janice, Loving, Timothy J., Stowell, Jeffrey R. Marlarkey, William B., Lemeshow, Stanley. Hostile Marital Interactions, Proinflammatory Cytokine Production, and Wound Healing. *Archives of General Psychiatry*, December, 2005; 62: 1377-1384.

Lawson, Christine. *Understanding the Borderline Mother* (Northvale, New Jersey: Jacob Aronson and Co., 2000).

Levine, Stephen. *Embracing the Beloved: Relationship as a Path of Awakening* (New York: Anchor Books, 1995).

Ludeman, Kate and Erlandson, Eddie. *Alpha Male Syndrome* (Boston: Harvard Business School Press, 2006).

Macchievelli, Niccolo; Godwin, Rufus and Soutino, Paul. *The Prince* (New York: Amherst, 1996).

Nathanson, Donald. "Understanding Emotion: New Theories, New Therapy," *Psychiatric Annals*, Volume 23, Number 10 (October, 1993).

Nathanson, Donald. *Shame and Pride: Affect, Sex, and the Birth of the Self* (New York: Norton and Company, Inc. 1992).

Newberg, Andrew; D'Aquili, Engene and Rause, Vince. *Why God Won't Go Away* (New York: Ballantine Books, 2001).

Peck, Scott. *People of the Lie: The Hope for Healing Human Evil* (New York: Touchstone, 1998).

Polti, Georges. *The Thirty-Six Dramatic Situations* (Franklin Ohio: James Knapp Reeve, 1921).

Real, Terrence. *I Don't Want to Talk About It: Overcoming the Secret Legacy of Male Depression* (New York: Fireside, 1997).

Real, Terrence. *How Can I Get Through to You? Closing the Intimacy Gap Between Men and Women* (New York: Fireside, 2002).

Real, Terrence. *The New Rules of Marriage* (New York: Ballantine Books, 2007).

Rieff, Phillip. *Charisma* (New York: Pantheon Books, 2007)

Ronningstam, Elsa F. *Narcissistic Personality* (Oxford, UK: Oxford University Press, 2005).

Smith, Manuel J. *When I Say No, I Feel Guilty* (New York: Dial Press, 1979.)

Stone, Hal and Stone, Siddra. *Embracing Ourselves; The Voice Dialogue Manual* (Novata, California: New World Library, 2001).

Sun Tzu. *The Illustrated Art of War* (Boston and London: Shambala, 1998).

Torgersen, et al. (2000) A twin study of personality disorders. *Comprehensive Psychiatry,* 41(6), 416-425.

Wallerstein, Judith and Blakeslee, Sandra. *The Good Marriage: How and Why Love Lasts* (New York: Houghton Mifflin Co., 1995)

Weiss, M., Zelkowitz, P., Feldman, R., Vogel, J., Heyman, M., Paris, J. "Psychopathology in Offspring of Mothers with Borderline Personality Disorder: A Pilot Study." *Canadian Journal of Psychiatry* (41, pp. 285-290, 1996).

The Who, *Tommy*, "Pinball Wizard" (1969).

INDEX

C